STEVE BLAMIRES

SKYLIGHT PRESS

First published in Great Britain in 2012 by Skylight Press,
210 Brooklyn Road, Cheltenham, Glos GL51 8EA

Designed and typeset by Rebsie Fairholm
Publisher: Daniel Staniforth

www.skylightpress.co.uk

Printed and bound in Great Britain by Lightning Source, Milton Keynes
Typeset in Adobe Caslon Pro. Titles set in HoneyBee.

British Library Cataloguing in Publication Data.
A catalogue record for this book is available from the British Library.

ISBN 978-1-908011-59-6

To Jenny
Mo Leannan

CONTENTS

INTRODUCTION

MUCH HAS BEEN written over the past several years on the subject of Faeries and the realm of Faery, whichever way you care to spell it. The mass of this is, by necessity, the words of human writers expressing what they believe to be the essence of the Faery tradition. This is all well and good but this can only ever be a stranger's interpretation of something they have never actually lived but only studied as an outsider looking in.

This present book inevitably falls somewhat into that category. I am human and I am writing about non-human beliefs, myths, deities, habits and practices. However my source material, the voluminous writings of Fiona Macleod, *has* come directly from the realm of Faery and through a pen guided by a Faery's hand. The authenticity of this source material can be seen from the quantity of new, previously unknown and unheard of myths, names, beliefs and details of the Realm of Faery itself. Some of this goes against the grain of contemporary belief and understanding of Faery and some aspects will no doubt be quite controversial in the minds of those already steeped in the subject. Be that as it may.

The published writings of the Faery Fiona Macleod come across as calm, steady and with a relaxed, take-your-time approach. Her private correspondence however, and her relationship with the human writer William Sharp, give a very different impression. These give a clear picture of a writer who was desperate to get her message out at all cost. And that cost turned out to be high, at least for William Sharp. She was on a mission to reveal to the human world as much as she could of her own Faery world and she had to do it as quickly as possible. I do not know why this should be. Perhaps her Faery sense of time differed from our human understanding of time. Perhaps, for some reason, she only had a limited amount of time allotted to her in which to achieve her goals. It does not matter why she was so persistent in driving William Sharp harder and harder to write down her teachings. That is how she was, that was her way.

The result was a thirteen year period when Victorian readers were swamped with novels, short stories, essays, plays, poems and copious magazine articles from this allegedly reclusive Scottish female writer.

During her lifetime her works were extremely popular but in 1905 when William Sharp died, and therefore so did the writings of Fiona Macleod, the public lost interest in her highly romantic tales, and to this day very few of her books have been reprinted. Now, in the 21st century, the sense of urgency coming from the Realm of Faery has returned. Anyone actively working this spiritual and magical system is probably well aware of this fact.

Over the past twenty or so years I have been fortunate enough to track down a substantial amount of Fiona Macleod material, published and unpublished, some of which I have managed to interpret from the original Faery point of view. This book is just a beginning in continuing the work of Fiona Macleod by making it once again available to the public to read, digest and, hopefully, understand and act upon. I hope you find it of interest.

Steve Blamires
Beacon, NY
January 2012

Chapter One

Biography of William Sharp

I deeply regret to inform you that ... Mr. William Sharp died quietly on Tuesday last, while on a visit to Castello di Maniace, Bronte, Sicily... Mr. Sharp was the author of all the works which have appeared under the name of Fiona Macleod.

FROM 1893 UNTIL 1905 the Victorian public was enthralled by the writings of the mysterious Fiona Macleod; writings that dealt mainly with life and love in the distant Highlands and Islands of Scotland. She quickly became so popular that there was an increasing demand from her readers to know more of this Scottish gentlewoman, but it turned out she was a shy, secretive person who shunned publicity and never gave interviews. Her entry in *Who's Who* for 1900 said simply:

"Macleod, Miss Fiona; author. Publications: Pharais, A Romance of the Isles 1894; The Mountain Lovers 1895; The Sin-Eater 1896; The Laughter of Peterkin 1897; and (in verse) From the Hills of Dream 1896. Collective Edition of the Celtic Tales from The Sin-Eater and Washer of the Ford, with others added, in 3 Volumes, Spiritual Tales, Barbaric Tales and Tragic Romances 1897. Forthcoming: an Historic Jacobite Romance; a new volume of short tales; and The Children of Danu (three prose Celtic dramas). Recreations: sailing, hill-walking, listening. Address: c/o Miss Rea, The Columbia Literary Agency, 9 Mill Street, Conduit Street, W."

This was not sufficient information for her readers and the literary critics of the day, but William Sharp, who claimed to be her cousin and literary agent, occasionally gave out more information to appease the pleas for detail and photographs. For example, he supplied the entry that appeared in *The North American Review* of October 1902, which says,

> *"Fiona Macleod published her first book in 1894, and since then there has been much speculation as to her personality, which has resulted in a number of myths, more or less amusing and absurd. The changing rumour went that she was William Sharp, that she was Mrs. Sharp, that she was the daughter of the late Dr. Norman Macleod, that she was Nora Hopper and W.B. Yeats in unison, that she was a syndicate of young Celtic authors, that she was a Fleet Street journalist, that she was Irish and her real name was Charles O'Connor, and even that she was Maud Gonne. Miss Macleod comes of an old, Highland, Catholic family of that name. She was born in the Southern Hebrides, and much of her childhood was passed in the Outer Hebrides or in the Inner Hebrides and the West Highlands of Scotland. The island of Innisron in her first romance, 'Pharais,' is believed to be a remote island where in childhood she spent many summers. So, too, certain incidents in the portraiture of the heroine Lora occurring in the same romance are, to some extent, founded upon her own personal experience. During the past eight years, Miss Macleod has wielded a busy pen. In addition to the romance already mentioned, she has published, among others, the following works: 'The Mountain Lovers,' 'The Sin-Eater,' 'The Washer of the Ford,' 'Green Fire,' 'From the Hills of Dream,' 'The Dominion of Dreams,' 'The Divine Adventure,' 'The Immortal Hour,' 'Trostan and Yseul.'"*

Note that this emphasises more who she is not rather than who she actually is.

On rare occasions Fiona Macleod would respond directly to a letter from an inquisitive reader who wished to know more of her, her family and life in the remote Gaelic speaking areas of Scotland. A typical reply would be, *"I was born more than a thousand years ago, in the remote region of Gaeldom known as the Hills of Dream. There I have lived the better part of my life; my father's name was Romance, and that of my mother was Dream. I have no photograph of their abode, which is just under the quicken-arch immediately west of the sunset rainbow. You will easily find it. Nor can I send you a photograph of myself. My last fell among the dew-wet heather, and is now doubtless lining the cells of the wild bees. All this authentic information I gladly send you."* We have no record of how the recipients of such a reply reacted!

However the final and only true statement made by William Sharp concerning Fiona Macleod and her wonderful writings came after his death on December 12th 1905. William Sharp had been a noted writer in his own right and his wife, Elizabeth, immediately sent telegrams to the newspapers of the day informing them of her husband's death. She also informed William's lover and inspiration, Edith Wingate Rinder, of his passing and she in turn sent telegrams to William's closest friends. That short message said,

Dec. 14, 1905

Dear Sirs,

I deeply regret to inform you that from a telegram received in the night from Mrs. William Sharp I learn that Mr. William Sharp died quietly on Tuesday last, while on a visit to Castello di Maniace, Bronte, Sicily. Mr. Sharp's health has caused concern for a long time, and for the past six winters he has been abroad. Mrs. William Sharp further expressly authorizes me to disclose that Mr. Sharp was the author of all the works which have appeared under the name of Fiona Macleod. I beg that you will regard this communication as private until to-morrow morning, when notices will appear in the papers.

Yours truly,

Edith Wingate Rinder

So, finally, after the death of William Sharp the truth about Fiona Macleod was revealed. He had indeed been the author of all the Fiona Macleod works despite his consistent and strenuous denials for the past thirteen years. Why did he do this? The use of a *nom-de-plume* was not uncommon and the adoption of a female name by a male writer was not unheard of either. Why did he put himself in a situation of having to permanently lie to even his closest and dearest friends and why take the constant risk of being exposed, all for the sake of a pen name? The answer is that whereas he knew it was true that it was he who committed the words of Fiona Macleod to writing he was also fully aware that he was not their author. To understand this it is necessary to examine the short life of William Sharp.

Some years after his death Elizabeth Sharp published her biography of her late husband, *William Sharp/Fiona Macleod: A Memoir*, and since then there have been a few discussions of the phenomenon of Fiona Macleod in obscure journals and academic papers, but none of these give the full story of who Fiona Macleod was or why William Sharp became the vehicle for her expression. In an attempt to correct this matter I published a full biography of William Sharp in 2008 under the title *The Little Book of the Great Enchantment* (RJ Stewart Books, PO Box 802, Arcata, CA 95518), which happens to also be the name of a book that Fiona referred to on several occasions in her own writings. Below I give a short account of his life and death for readers not familiar with either William Sharp or Fiona Macleod, in order to clarify what could otherwise be some confusing references throughout the remainder of this book.

William Sharp was born on September 12th 1855 in Central Scotland in the town of Paisley, near Glasgow. His father was in the banking business and the family was comfortably off. He was the eldest of seven children and for the earlier part of his life a nurse, Barbara, from the Hebrides, raised him. She was a native Gaelic speaker and taught the young William the Gaelic language and told him many of the old Celtic and Gaelic tales, songs and poems from her far northern home. In his later years he recalled, "When I was a child I used to throw offerings – small coins, flowers, shells, even a newly caught trout, once a treasured flint arrow-head – into the sea loch by which we lived. My Hebridean nurse had often told me of Shony, a mysterious sea-god, and I know I spent much time in wasted adoration: a fearful worship, not unmixed with disappointment and some anger. Not once did I see him. I was frightened time after time, but the sudden cry of a heron, or the snort of a pollack chasing the mackerel, or the abrupt uplifting of a seal's head became over-familiar, and I desired terror and could not find it by the shore. Inland, after dusk, there was always the mysterious multitude of shadow. There, too, I could hear the wind leaping and growling. But by the shore I never knew any dread, even in the darkest night. The sound and company of the sea washed away all fears." This early fascination with the sea would prove to be important in his later years as we shall see throughout this book.

He was a frail child and would suffer from chronic ill-health throughout his life. During the summer months the family would holiday in the mainland of the west of Scotland and often on the islands of the Inner Hebrides. Here William befriended an old fisherman named Seumas Macleod, and Seumas continued William's education in the Gaelic language and in the folklore, customs and traditions of the Gaelic speaking Highlanders and Islanders of those remote regions of Scotland. These early influences of Barbara and Seumas would later become extremely important for the development of Fiona Macleod and her writings.

He was an intelligent child and was given a good education but he was more interested in roaming the Highlands and Islands than he was in his academic studies. As a result much of his early life after finishing at Glasgow University was spent moving restlessly from one job to another, barely making enough money to live. This was a pattern that would stay with him for the rest of his life. At the age of twenty-nine he married his cousin Elizabeth Amelia Sharp, to whom he had been secretly engaged for nine years. This was another pattern that would manifest throughout his life – secrets, lots of them. Elizabeth encouraged him in his desire to be a writer, and through some social connections of his family he managed to involve himself in the circle of writers, artists and Bohemians that flourished in London where he was now living. He was in his element.

His written output was prolific but his talent was not great. He did manage to have several pieces published and he soon found a knack for biography. It was not long before the name of William Sharp was being mentioned outwith his own social and literary circle. All the time though he was on the move, barely managing to scrape by financially and suffering from several serious ailments and debilitating conditions.

Things took a life-changing turn in 1891 when he met Edith Wingate Rinder while spending the winter in Italy. He had met this attractive young lady before on a few fleeting social occasions back in London but their meeting this time in the Italian countryside near Rome turned into a passionate and life-long love affair. William had only been married to Elizabeth for a few years and Edith had only been married to her husband, Frank, for a few months, but it was clear they felt within their hearts that they were meant for each other. But this was no secret affair. Elizabeth Sharp and Frank Rinder both knew of their respective spouses' involvement with each other and accepted it as necessary and even a thing to be encouraged.

The reason for this unusual behaviour, especially in Victorian times, was because shortly after the love affair began William Sharp started to write under the name of Fiona Macleod. The inspiration for this was the torrent of emotion his love for Edith Wingate Rinder had unleashed, and it was obvious that what was happening regarding Fiona Macleod was unique, very important and something that had to be encouraged and nurtured. It soon became clear that although William was physically putting pen to paper he was not the author of the material being written. The style and subject matter of this burst of new creativity by Fiona Macleod was totally different from the writing style of William Sharp. When the truth was finally revealed after his death, many literary critics of the day refused to believe that William Sharp could have been responsible for the writings of Fiona Macleod because of their totally different styles. During the time Fiona was writing, William was continuing to write under his own name and it soon became apparent that he could only write as William Sharp when he was with his wife Elizabeth and could only write under the Fiona Macleod name when with his lover Edith. For the rest of his life William would move between the two women, as the muse, and his frail health, demanded.

However this was no ordinary literary device intended to sell books. William, Edith and Elizabeth all knew that Fiona Macleod was a person, an entity, a consciousness – call her what you will – in her own right. William never fully understood what was happening to him but he did accept without doubt that Fiona Macleod was a real, sentient being who had chosen him to be the vehicle for her writings; writings that are still of great importance today. So sure was William in his belief of the independent existence of Fiona Macleod that he would refer to her as "*our child*" when speaking of her to Elizabeth, and he was convinced she would 'die' if the secret of his connection with her was ever revealed. This is why he spent the last thirteen years of his life strenuously denying that he or any other person was Fiona Macleod, and why he made up fragments of her 'life' to satisfy the ever-swelling calls for information on this sensational new author, whenever he was put under pressure to do so. But it is clear from his own notebooks, private correspondence and the statements of close friends who were 'in the know' that William never knew what Fiona was going to write next, where her ideas came from, how characters would develop, etc. He was as fascinated by her writing as was the rest of the Victorian public.

Fiona's popularity soon brought correspondence from important people of the day such as the Irish poet, writer and senator William Butler Yeats. He saw her as an important figure in the Celtic Twilight movement of the 1890s and as a leading spokesperson in the struggle for Irish and Scottish independence and cultural recognition. This clearly brought even more problems for William Sharp who had to contend with not only his own correspondence but now also with the increasing correspondence from admirers of Fiona and her work. He also constantly had to come up with new and plausible excuses why she could not accept invitations for interviews, social events etc. The physical, emotional and spiritual effort of maintaining a double literary output, dealing with two completely separate sets of correspondence, providing enough detail regarding Fiona as to satisfy curiosity but not enough to allow verification, and the need to keep the secret hidden, all contributed to a steady decline in his already weak health.

So it was that while spending the winter with his friend the Duke of Bronte in Sicily, William Sharp finally departed this life on December 12th 1905 at the age of fifty. For some years after his death Elizabeth tried to keep in touch with him through mediums and séances. Whenever Elizabeth asked her spirit contacts about Fiona the reply was always: "*Fiona is no more.*" William had been right in his belief that once the secret was revealed Fiona would die.

Elizabeth Sharp and Edith Wingate Rinder remained good friends until Elizabeth died in the 1930s. Edith passed away in the 1960s at the age of ninety-three. Elizabeth's eagerly awaited biography of her late husband came out several years after his death and despite being a substantial volume it says very little about the whole phenomenon of Fiona Macleod. Elizabeth simply states: "*The name flashed ready made to my husband's mind.*" Edith never wrote or commented on her lover following his death, and she took what secrets she knew of the nature of Fiona Macleod with her to her grave. The literature-loving public forgot about Fiona Macleod and to this day very few of her works have ever been reprinted. But they are well worth seeking out and I make no apology for quoting them at length in this discussion on the deeper meanings behind her romantic, tragic, sometimes happy and often sad, but always highly descriptive stories, poems, plays and essays.

Although Fiona is no more, the valuable information that she revealed is still providing the serious student of the Realm of Faery with more and more information, practical suggestions and spiritual truths. What follows in this volume is but a scratch on a very deep surface. I encourage all my readers to widen and deepen that scratch with their own researches, experiments, meditations and practical spiritual and magical investigations.

Chapter Two

ҒIONA'S COMMENTS
ON HER OWN WRITING

These hours of beauty have meant so much to me, somewhat in the writing, but much more in the long, incalculable hours and days out of which the writing has risen like the blue smoke out of woods, that I want to share them with others, who may care for the things written of as you and I care for them, and among whom may be a few who, likewise, will be moved to garner from each day of the eternal pageant one hour of unforgettable beauty.

THE FAERY BEING who took the name Fiona Macleod and who worked through the Scottish writer William Sharp had one purpose in life – a desire to reveal to the human world as much as possible of her native Realm of Faery. To this end she spent thirteen years struggling with the problems of putting into human language the important concepts and abstract beliefs from another world and another race that she felt compelled to reveal. It was a mammoth and highly ambitious task. She probably succeeded more than we realise for it is more our failure to recognise the importance of what she said than it was her inability to put it across that has caused much to go unnoticed and under-appreciated. Fortunately today in the 21st century we have well over one hundred years of research and study of her works to draw upon. However only a few dedicated researchers and students of Faery lore have taken the time and effort to tease out the Faery gems that are still to be found woven into the lines and verse of her writings. I am pleased to be able to contribute to this body of knowledge through this present book.

Before entering into a detailed examination of Fiona's Faery lore I should stress to the reader unfamiliar with her work that nowhere in her writings did she state that her purpose was to reveal the Faery tradition to humankind. She did not write text books on the Faery tradition, nor did she give out specific instructions. All of her writings can be taken at face value and enjoyed for what they are: short stories, poems, plays, essays etc, centred mainly on life, love and death in the Gaelic-speaking Highlands and Islands of Scotland. But woven into these romantic, fantastic and at times horrific tales are many, many threads that when teased out and woven together in a coherent form reveal the multi-coloured shimmering tapestry of the Faery tradition. The purpose of this present book is to help you find the keys that are necessary to unlock this ancient and fascinating tradition.

First though let us look at how Fiona herself regarded her task and what her opinions and feelings were on the writing she produced. To this end, wherever possible throughout this book I use Fiona's own words on any given subject and follow those with pertinent comments, observations and suggestions of my own and others. Much of what she said in her many books, magazine articles, essays, poems and plays was reprinted, in various combinations, several times during her life, resulting in a confusing mass of repetition, deletion and amendment. However there is substantially more material that has never been reprinted, plus there are literally thousands of personal letters, postcards and telegrams that reveal much of her own personal nature that cannot be found anywhere else. These obscure and long-neglected comments, opinions, thoughts and ideas often contain snippets of great value to the student of Faery lore. I have been fortunate to track down a great deal of this esoteric material and I am pleased to make it available in the following pages, most of it for the first time. I believe that Fiona always wanted everything to be revealed and made as available as possible both during her lifetime and after her death but, until now, this has not happened. The reason for this was mainly due to some highly delicate aspects of William Sharp's personal life that his widow, Elizabeth Sharp, managed to conceal after his death in 1905 and until long after her own death in 1932. These details can be found in *The Little Book of the Great Enchantment,* my biography of William Sharp and Fiona Macleod.

First, here is an excerpt from a letter Fiona sent to an American admirer in April 1897, just three years after her first book appeared in the UK. In this long letter she reveals more of herself than she usually did. Later, as the requests for information became more frequent and more demanding, she learned to say little and stay in the background. The important part says,

> *"There are some writers who dwell apart, in every sense of the word: and I am one of these. My wishes and my tastes, as well as certain exigencies in my private circumstances, incline me towards a greater privacy or isolation than suits that ethic of publicity which prevails and is to me so undignified and even distressing: and hence have arisen many strange rumours about me and as to 'who I am' etc. And in like manner, even those who know me say that I am a survival from a remote past, and not a proper modern at all. This is not quite true, for I believe in one intensity of emotion above all others, namely the intensity of this brief flame of life in the heart and the brain, an intensity no one can have who does not account the hours of every day as the vanishing pawns in that tragic came of chess for ever being played between Time and Eternity. All the same, I have mentally ever been impassioned for the past and so it is that I find myself, both in the inner and outer life, much aloof from my fellows. I find in the close and intimate communion with nature, which is so much more possible away from towns — and I live truly only when I am in the remote Isles or among the mountains of Argyll — a solace and inspiration which come to me much attenuated through the human medium. Perhaps this is because, though young in years, I have a capacity for sorrow and regret which has come to me through my Celtic ancestry out of a remote lost world: because, indeed, I have myself walked the blind way between Joy and Sorrow and been led now by the one now by the other. But do not think I am a melancholy person. I am not, in the ordinary sense. I am young, and life has given me some of her rarest gifts, and I am grateful: and, when my hour comes, shall be ready, having lived. Not even in my vision of life am I melancholy. All the same, I am, as you discern, saturated with the gloom and strangeness of life from one vital point of view: and am ever aware of the menace of the perpetual fugitive shadow of Destiny. It is summed up in a dream I had once, lying among the grassy dunes of Iona: a dream wherein I heard a voice saying in Gaelic that the three Dominions or Powers were 'The Living God, the Dying World, and the mysterious Race of Man,' and that behind each gleamed the shadowy eyes of Destiny."*

This reveals a good deal of her inner processes and gives just a glimpse of her as a person but it is calm, collected and devoid of deep passion or emotion. However in her pivotal essay *Iona* the normally calm and collected Fiona Macleod displayed a rare passion. Of this essay she once said, *"I have never written anything mentally so spiritually autobiographical. Strange as it may seem it is almost all literal reproduction of actuality with only some dates and names altered."* I will quote from this important piece frequently throughout this book. Here is an excerpt that displays her strong feelings for the value of the old Faery beliefs and traditions.

> *"In the maelstrom of the cities the old race perishes, drowns. How common the foolish utterance of narrow lives, that all these old ways of thought are superstitious. To have a superstition is, for these, a worse ill than to have a shrunken soul. I do not believe in spells and charms and foolish incantations, but I think that ancient wisdom out of the simple and primitive heart of an older time is not an ill heritage; and if to believe in the power of the spirit is to be superstitious, I am well content to be of the company that is now forsaken."*

She then goes on to quote an old Gaelic rune that mentions the arrows of the slim fairy women, and she comments,

> *"And I — do I believe in that? At least it will be admitted that it is worth a belief; it is a pleasant dream; it is a gate into a lovely world; it is a secret garden, where are old sweet echoes; it has the rainbow-light of poetry. Is it not poetry? And I — oh yes, I believe it, that superstition: a thousand-fold more real is it, more believable, than that coarse-tongued, ill-mannered, boorish people, desperate in slovenly pleasure. For that will stay, and they will go. And if I am wrong, then I will rather go with it than stay with them. And yet — surely, surely the day will come when this sordidness of life as it is so often revealed to us will sink into deep waters, and the stream become purified, and again by its banks be seen the slim fairy women of health and beauty and all noble and dignified things."*

On a slightly more autobiographical note, Fiona once made a reference to having a foster sister. This may not mean much to present day readers but up until the early years of the 20th century in the Gaelic-speaking areas of the Highlands and Islands the relationships between foster children and their foster parents, and between foster children and their siblings, was considered to be of a stronger bond than that between parents and their biological children. In an article entitled 'From the Hebrid Isles' published in *Harpers Magazine*, December 1895, she says, *"I had been spending some weeks with Alasdair McIan and his wife Silis (who was my foster-sister), at their farm of Ardoch, high in a remote hill country."* This states unambiguously that Silis was Fiona Macleod's foster sister and it is safe to assume that there would have been a very close bond between them. The name Silis crops up again in a story called *The Archer* and I discuss this important short story in detail in my book *The Little Book of the Great Enchantment* as it was based an actual incidents that were occurring at that time in the life of William Sharp and his lover Edith Wingate Rinder. In the story, Silis has to choose between staying with her husband and leaving with his friend who had confessed a love for her. Silis in the story is Edith Wingate Rinder who at that time had to decide whether to remain with her husband Frank Rinder or leave him for William Sharp. As I make clear in *The Little Book of the Great Enchantment*, Edith Wingate Rinder was the catalyst that enabled Fiona Macleod to 'come through' William Sharp. So, by referring to Silis as her foster sister, Fiona is making it very clear that she had a particularly strong bond with the human Edith Wingate Rinder and acknowledged the important role she played in enabling her to reveal her Faery lore.

But to return to Fiona's more general comments – her essay *Iona* contains this little statement on a phenomenon common in the Highlands and Islands – spontaneous clairvoyance or, to give it the local name, the second-sight:

> *"There is something strangely beautiful in most of these 'second-sight' stories... The faculty itself is so apt to the spiritual law that one wonders why it is so set apart in doubt. It would, I think, be far stranger if there were no such faculty... That I have cause to believe is perhaps too personal a statement, and is of little account; but in that interior wisdom, which is no longer the flicker of one little green leaf but the light and sound of a forest, of which the leaf is a part, I know that to be true, which I should as soon doubt as that the tide returns or that the sap rises or that the dawn is a ceaseless flashing light beneath the circuit of the star. Spiritual logic demands it."*

Her essay *Iona* was not, however, her first publication. Her first two published books were *Pharais: A Romance of the Isles* and *The Mountain Lovers*, both of which were full-length novels. About these books she once said, *"You will find more of me in 'Pharais' than in anything I have written. Let me add that you will find 'The Mountain Lovers' more elemental still, while simpler ..."*

Her comment that there is more of her to be found in *Pharais* than in anything else is at the same time interesting and disturbing. It is interesting in that here is a clear statement that if you study this book you will learn much of her nature; but it is disturbing, as the subject of the book – madness, attempted suicides, infant mortality, loneliness and loss – would imply that Fiona Macleod must be a very depressed and perhaps depressing personality. If this is the case, does it mean that this is typical of Faery beings, and if so, does that mean contact with the Faeries may bring about a corresponding depression in the student? We shall address these rather disturbing possibilities frequently throughout this book, as they are ones that will recur from time to time as we delve deeper into Faery lore and mythology, and we cannot sweep them under the spiritual carpet. First, though, I should point out that Fiona was later to revise her opinions of these first two books.

In 1900, six years after *Pharais* and *The Mountain Lovers* had been published, her attitude to them had changed significantly. In a letter dated May 4th 1900, to her friend the Celtic scholar Ernest Rhys, she said:

> *"They are books at which I look sometimes with dread … Can you understand that when 'Pharais' was published I would have given anything to recall it, partly because of the too much suffering there expressed, but mainly because of that 'Cry of Women,' which nevertheless had brought so many strange and sorrowful letters, and made many unexpected friends."*

One reader who was much affected by the negativity of Fiona's early writings was the writer Katharine Tynan, who said,

> *"There is much that is darkening and dreadful in Fiona Macleod's work even when it is most remarkable from a literary point of view. 'The Dan-na-Ron', 'The Ninth Wave', 'The Sin-Eater', have all to my mind a dreadful power of depressing the reader … That they should have the power to depress is a tribute to their literary quality. I may say that my first experience with 'Pharais' left me with a sense of dislike and fear for the work of Fiona Macleod. I felt that it was not good reading for the sensitive and imaginative … Neither William Sharp nor Fiona Macleod brought into their work any hint of the saving sense of humour. To be sure Fiona was always writing at the top of her voice, in a passion which had no room for the ludicrous."*

Fiona's revelation that she regretted writing *Pharais* and *The Mountain Lovers* is because by 1900 she had started to better understand the ways of this world that were unknown and totally unfamiliar to her in 1893-94 when she wrote those books. She wisely made a conscious decision to move away from using the subject of human emotions and interaction as the vehicles for her Faery teachings. There is a definite change of emphasis in her work from the late 1890s onwards. Her initial burst of output, from 1893 until around 1897-98, was these first two novels and a flood of short stories and narratives dealing with the life, trials and tribulations of the Gaelic Highlander. Many of these deal with depression, madness, loneliness, drowning and so forth, while at the same time describing a physically beautiful environment in which her tragic characters lived. By 1898 it is noticeable that she had started to move away from short stories and novels dealing with these darker aspects of human life. Instead she started to express her Faery lore in essays, poems and commentaries on the beauty and powers of the Green World, on spirituality, on the bigger picture as opposed to the complications of the lives of her individual characters. After four or five years of writing and experiencing our world she began to understand how better to put across to her readers what she was so desperate to reveal in a way that was not as threatening or depressing as her earlier work had been.

During her lifetime several people commented on the fact that Fiona's writings can be split into these three separate phases or periods. For example, William Sharp's widow Elizabeth commented that Fiona's output, "*... passed from the youth in 'Pharais' and 'The Mountain Lovers', through the mature manhood of 'The Barbaric Tales and Tragic Romances' to the greater serenity of later contemplative life in 'The Divine Adventure,' 'The Winged Destiny' and 'Where the Forest Murmurs'.*" This threefold change in style and subject is useful to keep in mind when studying, as opposed to simply reading, her works. The early material is in essence much stronger and more powerful because Fiona, in her inexperience of human understanding, laid out her Faery revelations in a way that we were not ready for. After her initial burst of enthusiasm was met with comments like those of Katharine Tynan, she tamed things down considerably and restructured her material in a way that was gentler and more acceptable to Victorian mores and expectations.

These first offerings were so popular that soon the public was demanding to know more of this mysterious Highland lady. From the start, William Sharp knew he would need to be very careful in what he revealed of his 'cousin,' as he claimed her to be. If he were too specific there would be the chance of the truth being uncovered. If he were too vague then that would only generate more questions and inquisitive minds. It was a charade he would struggle with for the last thirteen years of his life. Fiona, however, dealt with the requests for personal information much more simply. Early in her career she said,

> *"By blood I am part Celt, and partly so by upbringing, by Spirit wholly so ... One day I will tell you of the strange old mysteries of earlier days I have part learned, part divined, and other things of the spirit ... I resent too close identification with the so-called Celtic renaissance. If my work is to depend solely on its Gaelic connection, then let it go, as go it must. My work must be beautiful in itself — Beauty is a Queen and must be served as a Queen."*

Here she makes it clear that she does not want to be labelled exclusively under the category 'Celtic.' This was very much the rage in the late Victorian era when a veritable flood of books dealing with all aspects of Celtic history, mythology and languages was unleashed on the Victorian public. Right from the start Fiona made it clear that she did not consider herself or her writings as part of that movement.

The interesting comment in this quotation is, *"One day I will tell you of the strange old mysteries of earlier days I have part learned, part divined, and other things of the spirit..."* This sums up her whole reason for manifesting in this world through William Sharp – to reveal the Faery lore, or the *"strange old mysteries of earlier days"* as she has it, *as Faery lore* and not just as yet another outpouring of in-vogue Celtic tidbits. The final sentence in this quotation, *"My work must be beautiful in itself — Beauty is a Queen and must be served as a Queen"* gives a very strong hint as to its Faery origin. Today most people are familiar with the 'fairy tales' they heard in childhood and, as adulthood progressed, either forgot them or considered them of no value. Many of these ancient folktales did at one time contain valuable Faery lore but through the passing of time this has been garbled, corrupted, edited out or simply forgotten. Apart from beauty. A rereading of childhood fairy tales reminds us just how much emphasis is placed on beauty in these tales. The story *Sleeping Beauty* of course springs to mind but if we delve further back into early medieval literature, and especially the huge corpus of tales concerning King Arthur, it will be found that the theme of beauty, and beautiful people, especially women, recurs time and time again. It is, if you like, a 'code word' for places or persons from the Realm of Faery. Take note of this. We shall look more closely at the theme of Faery Beauty and other Faery code words in later chapters.

Most of Fiona's Faery revelations are in her books and magazine articles, but there is also much to be found in her private letters to correspondents with whom she had empathy and with whom she felt she could be frank and open. A good deal more is tucked away in long dedications and forewords to her books and essays. I am sure most of her readers did read these opening paragraphs but I am also sure that in their haste to read the main chapters of her stories many people missed the valuable clues and comments buried therein.

One such important passage is to be found in the dedication to her collection of essays called *Where the Forest Murmurs*. This dedication is to Mr. P. Anderson Graham, who had encouraged Fiona to submit her material to the popular Victorian magazine *Country Life*. What she said to him in this dedication tells us something of her Faery notion of writing for humans.

> *"To whom so fittingly as you could I inscribe this book? It was you who suggested it; you who in 'Country Life' published at intervals, longer or shorter as the errant spirit of composition moved me, the several papers which make it one book; you without whose encouragement and good counsel this volume would probably not have been written. Then, perchance, it might have gone to that Y-Brasil Press in the Country of the Young wherefrom are issued all the delightful books which, though possible and welcome in Tir-na-n'Og, are unachieved in this more difficult world, except in dreams and hopes. It would be good to have readers among the kindly Shee ... do not the poets there know an easy time, having only to breathe their thought onto a leaf and to whisper their music to a reed, and lo the poem is public from the caverns of Tir-fo-tuinn to the hills of Fleathanas! ... but, till one gets behind the foam yonder, the desire of the heart is for comrades here. These hours of beauty have meant so much to me, somewhat in the writing, but much more in the long, incalculable hours and days out of which the writing has risen like the blue smoke out of woods, that I want to share them with others, who may care for the things written of as you and I care for them, and among whom may be a few who, likewise, will be moved to garner from each day of the eternal pageant one hour of unforgettable beauty."*

(Note the use of the word 'beauty'.)

The collection of essays *Where the Forest Murmurs* was written quite late in Fiona's career, between 1903 and 1905, and by that time she had found a style that allowed her to reveal her Faery lore without the dark undertones that were so dominant in her first two novels. Prior to then she had tried different styles, subjects and vocabulary but never quite managed to make things as clear as she would have wished. From this paragraph above it is clear that by this late period Fiona had found her style and form of expression and thoroughly enjoyed putting pen to paper and allowing her store of Faery lore and mythology to flow out for all and sundry to read. This excerpt is also a typical example of her at times flowery language and her easy mixing of Gaelic and English. The place names she gives are all from the Realm of Faery. *Y-Brasil* is an old Celtic name for the Otherworld or Realm of Faery; *Tir-na-n'Og* is from the Gaelic language and means 'land of youth' or, as she says in the phrase before, 'the Country of the Young'; *Tir-fo-tuinn* is also Gaelic and means the 'land under the waves,' another expression for the Realm of Faery. The place name *Fleathanas* is a word found in some early Gaelic Christian writings that refer to Heaven being an island somewhere in the west. This is clearly not standard Christian doctrine and is a mixing of the pre-Christian Faery belief and the later teachings of the Church – a theme that Fiona would return to time and time again. Knowing this helps to uncover a deeper level to Fiona's writings. Whenever she related events as happening in any of these locations she was telling us that they were in the Realm of Faery, not this world. A small point perhaps but one that starts to open Faery doors that the causal reader will not even notice are there.

The segment that says "*... the Country of the Young wherefrom are issued all the delightful books which ... are unachieved in this more difficult world, except in dreams and hopes ...*" tells us that books are known in the Realm of Faery but, naturally, they differ from the books of our world. This sentence also hints at the importance of paying attention to dreams and hopes, for these are nothing less than the beginnings of making real in this world the truths and teachings of Faery. This is important. Much Faery communication comes in the form of dreams and of sudden strong hopes, ideals or ambitions which, at the time, often go unrecognized and are lost in a moment when the logical, sterile mind of "*this more difficult world,*" as Fiona calls it, brushes them aside as being of no value. This is not to say that *all* dreams, hopes and ambitions are as a result of unrecognized Faery communication, far from it. The task of the earnest seeker after Faery lore is to learn how to discriminate between the fantasies created by nothing more than a dreaming mind and the much more valuable seed-ideas that are planted in the imagination by a Faery contact. Much of Fiona's writings deal with this more subtle aspect of learning all about Faery and how to interpret the wealth of actual Faery lore, belief, mythology and so forth she made available. In a sense, she not only gave us her Faery words but also the dictionaries and grammar books to translate and understand them. Her comment on dreams and hopes is just one such pointer.

The sentence that follows is interesting. *"It would be good to have readers among the kindly Shee … do not the poets there know an easy time, having only to breathe their thought onto a leaf and to whisper their music to a reed, and lo the poem is public from the caverns of Tir-fo-tuinn to the hills of Fleathanas!"* This tells us something of the nature of Faery 'books' and of the manner of Faery communication in general. The Faery writer or poet only has to think of their subject and it is made manifest throughout the Realm of Faery for those who choose to pick it up. Sometimes people of this world unconsciously pick up these air-borne Faery thoughts and commentaries, hence the comment above concerning the importance of dreams and hopes. Note that Fiona expresses a longing she knows cannot be fulfilled when she says *"It would be good to have readers among the kindly Shee …"* The Shee, or Sidhe, are the Faeries, and she reveals here that they do not and cannot read the books that she is producing for human edification. This shows that by the early 1900s she had become more adept at writing human books for human people and realised what a valuable teaching aid they are for us, but can never be so for her own kind.

One such Faery book that was issued from the Country of the Young is *The Little Book of the Great Enchantment* (the original, not my later book of the same name). Fiona drew on this book several times in her own writings and I discuss it in depth in my book of the same name, being the biography of William Sharp. When Fiona quoted from this and other Faery books, she spoke of them in a manner that implied she assumed her human readers were as familiar with them as they would be if she had quoted from Shakespeare, for example. It is important to note this. Fiona had a habit of mixing human and Faery lore together in one sentence, paragraph or even whole book with no attempt to point out which came from where. This holistic approach is a good thing once you have grasped the basics of Faery lore as it helps to unify it with your normal, every day human life and make them both one homogenous whole, as they should be. But until you have learned to pick out the Faery from the human lore it can be a confusing task to study her writings. Hopefully this book will go a long way to helping you learn the techniques of unravelling these valuable 'publications' from the Country of the Young.

There is a subtle but important point to note in the longing she expressed. It is nothing to do with the desire itself but with the fact that she refers to the Shee as being 'kindly.' In the Victorian and Edwardian eras, when this dedication was written, you would have been hard pressed to find anyone who would describe the Faeries as kind. Belief in Faeries was far more common and taken far more seriously by the public at large in those days than it is in our own. During the 1830s and 1840s at least one serious display on the subject of the latest research into faeries was exhibited every year at the annual exhibitions of both the Royal Academy and British Institution, both well respected scientific bodies. But that belief in Faeries also held the tenet that they were dangerous, malicious and should be avoided at all costs. Fiona commented on this in the opening note to her important play *The Immortal Hour* where she said,

> *"It should be added that with the ancient Gaels (and with the few today who have not forgotten or do not disdain the old wisdom) the Hidden People (the Sidhe or Shee; or Shee'an or Sheechun of the Isles) were great and potent, not small and insignificant beings. 'Mab' long ago was the terrible 'dark' queen, Maive (Medb Medbh, Mabh): and the still more ancient Puck was not a frolicsome spirit, but a shadowy and dreadful Power."*

Her poem *The Hills of Ruel* again expresses the sentiment that the Faeries are inherently cruel and a threat to both the living and the dead.

The Hills of Ruel

"Over the hills and far away" —
That is the tune I heard one day
When heather-drowsy I lay and listened
And watched where the stealthy sea-tide glistened.

Beside me there on the Hills of Ruel
An old man stooped and gathered fuel —
And I asked him this: if his son were dead,
As the folk in Glendaruel all said,
How could he still believe that never
Duncan had crossed the shadowy river.

Forth from his breast the old man drew
A lute that once on a rowan-tree grew:
And, speaking no words, began to play
"Over the hills and far away."

"But how do you know," I said, thereafter,
"That Duncan has heard the fairy laughter?
How do you know he has followed the cruel
Honey-sweet folk of the Hills of Ruel?"

"How do I know?" the old man said,
"Sure I know well my boy's not dead:
For late on the morrow they hid him, there
Where the black earth moistens his yellow hair,
I saw him alow on the moor close by,
I watched him low on the hillside lie,
An' I heard him laughin' wild up there,
An' talk, talk, talkin' beneath his hair —
For down o'er his face his long hair lay
But I saw it was cold and ashy grey.

Aye, laughin' and talkin' wild he was,
An' that to a Shadow out on the grass,
A Shadow that made my blood grow chill,
For never its like have I seen on the hill.
An' the moon came up and the stars grew white,
An' the hills grew black in the bloom o' the night,
An' I watched till the death-star sank in the moon
And the moonmaid fled with her flittermice shoon,
Then the Shadow that lay on the moorside there
Rose up and shook its wildmoss hair,
And Duncan he laughed no more, but grey
As the rainy dust of a rainy day.
Went over the hills and far away."

"Over the hills and far away"
That is the tune I heard one day.
O that I might too hear the cruel
Honey-sweet folk of the Hills of Ruel.

Note that despite the old man's bitter sentiments on the Faeries stealing his son, Fiona does not take this as a warning to stay clear of them but instead ends the poem by expressing a longing that she too might hear them! Fiona did more often than not speak of the Faeries in soft and sympathetic terms throughout her writings. This is understandable considering that she was speaking of her own people, but it was a new approach, a new point of view, for the Victorian reader. Consider the comments Alexander Carmichael collected in the late 1800s from the Gaelic-speaking people of the Highlands and Islands of Scotland that were published in his several volumes called *Carmina Gadelica*. Many of these runes, songs and sayings mention the Faeries but none express any sympathy for them or any longing to be near them. For example, Rune number 10 says,

> *Bless, O Chief of generous chiefs,*
> *Myself and everything anear me,*
> *Bless me in all my actions,*
> *Make Thou me safe forever,*
> *Make Thou me safe forever.*
>
> *From every brownie and ban-shee,*
> *From every evil wish and sorrow,*
> *From every nymph and water-wraith,*
> *From every fairy-mouse and grass-mouse,*
> *From every fairy-mouse and grass-mouse.*
>
> *From every troll among the hills,*
> *From every siren hard pressing me,*
> *From every ghoul within the glens,*
> *Oh! Save me till the end of my day.*
> *Oh! Save me till the end of my day.*

Rune number 262, called simply *Prayer,* says,

> *I pray and supplicate*
> *Cuibh and Columba,*
> *The Mother of my King,*
> *Brigit womanly,*

Michael militant,
High-king of the angels,
To succour and shield me
From each Faery on earth.

The runes from number 507 through to number 520 contain many warnings about taking a Faery lover and, especially, warnings about having children of mixed blood. Judging from the number of runes and prayers on this subject of inter-racial breeding it was clearly regarded as a serious threat that such things could happen. This is interesting. In her story *Faruane* Fiona gives exactly the same warnings to Faeries about consorting with humans. I give a full discussion on this in Chapter Seven.

Carmina Gadelica also has a section explaining that it is possible to outwit the Faeries in a battle of words and that as long as you stand fast the Faeries cannot win. One section in particular, page 513, says,

"A fairy woman came to where a mortal woman was nursing a little child. She stood stubbornly, stiffly, starkly, before the child, peering and staring at it straight in the face. At last she said:
'Comely is thy child, woman,' quoth the fairy woman.
'Comely is every lucky worldling,' said the nurse.
'Green is thy child, woman,' said the fairy woman.
'Green is the grass, but it grows,' said the nurse.
'White of skin is thy child, woman,' said the fairy woman.
'White of skin is the snow of the peaks,' said the nurse.
'Pretty and golden are thy child's locks, woman,' said the fairy woman.
'Pretty and golden is the daisy of the plain,' said the nurse.
'Sharp and cutting is thy tongue, woman,' said the fairy woman.
'It was never set to a grindstone,' said the nurse.
When the fairy woman saw that the mortal woman would not yield her an inch here nor there, down nor up, she turned the back of her head to her and departed by the way she had come, and never did herself nor any of her people come again upon that ground. Oh, she came not ever again that way, the black nor the white of her ever ever again."

So Fiona's insertion of the word *kindly* to describe the Faeries was strikingly unusual and set against a background amongst the common people of complete fear and rejection of anything to do with the Faeries.

This could have been a major stumbling block for her when it came to having her Faery teachings accepted by the Victorian public but her compelling literary style, and her intricately beautiful descriptive passages, especially those concerning the world of nature, helped greatly in nullifying what could otherwise have been a very negative reaction to her publications.

A small comment on Victorian society is appropriate here. The higher classes of society, such as William Sharp's family, were keen on participating in séances, and we know William Sharp attended séances, as did his wife following his death; but these people who unashamedly believed in the spirit world openly scoffed at a belief in Faeries. The rustic, lower class Victorians however ignored séances but kept their Faery beliefs very much alive. This all started to change though, and a belief in the Faeries by the well-to-do Victorians started to manifest and become acceptable at a time that was coincidental with the chipping away at the mysteries of the Bible by the new sciences, especially geology and palaeontology. While science was removing the mysteries of life by reducing everything to explainable phenomena, the intelligent people to whom these scientific rationales were directed were in fact turning to a belief in the Faeries for the simple reason that science still could *not* explain them. Humankind needs the mysterious and unexplained and Fiona Macleod gave just that.

Fiona used the dedications in her books almost like personal 'thank you' letters to friends, such as the dedication to Mr. P. Anderson Graham quoted above. In another personal dedication in the essay *Iona*, Fiona addresses the writer George Meredith and once again speaks of her own writings. Of these she says,

> *"Well I know that they do not give 'a rounded and complete portrait of the Celt.' It is more than likely that I could not do so if I tried, but I have not tried; not even to give 'a rounded and complete portrait' of the Gael, who is to the Celtic race what the Franco-Breton is to the French, a creature not without blitheness and humour, laughter-loving, indolent, steadfast, gentle, fierce, but above all attuned to elemental passions, to the poetry of nature, and wrought in every nerve and fibre by the gloom and mystery of his environment."*

When you delve deeply into Fiona Macleod's writings it soon becomes apparent that in some instances she is very precise and specific in her use of the terms 'Celt,' 'Gael' and 'Faery' – to us all quite clear and separate appellations – but in places these terms become blurred, merge one into another and appear to be synonymous. Many of her more confusing, obscure or unclear comments on Celts or Gaels actually make much more sense when the word Faery is substituted. This confusion was caused in part because the mythology, language and beliefs of the Celt and Gael both share a common link with those of the Realm of Faery. That is not to say that they are the same or totally interchangeable but they do bear enough similarity and common ground to make confusion a thing that can easily happen. In the last few years the serious study of Faery lore has increased but there has been a certain amount of careless and inaccurate mixing of Faery mythology and Celtic mythology based on the underlying belief that they are one and the same. This is not the case. The blame for much of this could be laid at Fiona's door as she was guilty of making statements and naming names allegedly from ancient Celtic belief that were in truth from Faery belief. This was not a careless error or deliberate deception on Fiona's part. It was solely due to her difficulty in making the separations between the two ancient traditions that we in our human world know and expect. Be careful when reading her work. When she states that such and such a thing is 'ancient Celtic' try substituting 'ancient Faery' and then it will probably be more accurate and more revealing.

For a period in the late 1890s Fiona was in frequent contact by letter with the Scottish writer and journalist John Macleay. In this correspondence she often commented on her latest publications and ideas, and these personal observations and critiques point out the writings that she felt were of special worth. For example, on 31st May 1899 she wrote,

> *"I greatly hope that you, one of my earliest and staunchest friends across the pen will care for 'The Dominion of Dreams'. To me it stands for my best work, as it is certainly the deepest and most mature: though I can well understand how its appeal must be limited. After all, I doubt if I really care for any work save that which tells imaginatively of imagination and spiritual emotion, or the old pagan life."*

This last sentence is very revealing. To most of her readers the appeal of her writings was the highly romantic subject matter, the tragic heroes and heroines, the descriptions of life in the remote Highlands and Islands plus the many and meticulous descriptions of the natural world. Yet here Fiona states quite clearly she cares naught for these things. What was important to her was the use of the imagination, the expression of spiritual emotion and the old pagan (for which read 'Faery') way of life.

The collection of short stories *The Dominion of Dreams* contains many good examples of how she managed to satisfy the romantic expectations of her readers while at the same time embodying within these tales the imaginative, spiritual and Faery lore that was the more important aspect for her. She mentioned this book again in another letter from 1899 to Edith Lyttleton in which she said,

> *"Many, because of the reputation I have been fortunate enough to win, such as it is, will read my shortly forthcoming book, 'The Dominion of Dreams,'... but how few will care much for it, how fewer still will really understand it, or the most intimate part of it. Yet, in a sense, if I may say so, it is a profoundly revelative book. Well, if it gains wide and sincere appreciation I shall be glad: if it should practically be ignored I shall be sorry: but, beyond that, I am indifferent. I know what I have tried to do: I know what I have done: I know the end to which I work: I believe in the sowers who will sow and the reapers who will reap, from some seed of the spirit in this book: and, knowing this, I have little heed of other considerations. Beauty, in itself, is my dream: and in some expression of it, in the difficult and subtle art of words, I have a passionate absorption."*

Once again, note the use of the word *beauty*. Several of the tales in this book give out a great deal of previously unknown Faery mythology, custom and belief but all couched within short stories that, superficially, do not appear to contain any deliberate higher meaning. Most interesting and revealing of these tales are *Dalua, By The Yellow Moonrock, Children of the Dark Star, The Amadan* and *The Birds of Emar*. The short story called *The Amadan* (The Fool) contains a Faery rune, later called *The Invocation of Peace*, which is of such great importance we shall examine it in detail later, in Chapter Eleven.

On 20th October 1899 she wrote to Mr. Macleay and commented on another of her forthcoming titles. *"I hope you will read 'The Divine Adventure', as it is called ... though this spiritual essay is more 'remote', i.e. unconventional and in a sense more 'mystical', than anything I have done. But it is out of my inward life."* This piece first appeared in the magazine *The Fortnightly Review* during November and December of 1899. It was later published in 1900 in book form along with several other important pieces, mainly the long essay *Iona*, and this collection of essays and short stories also reveals much Faery lore in its pages.

Earlier that year, on 8th June, she wrote to Mr. Macleay and said, *"But I don't 'go to the isles' for beauty. The isles — the past — the pagan wonder and mystery — <u>come to me</u>! It is what a writer <u>receives</u> that makes him or her. All art is from within. It is from what dies into one, and is reborn."* Almost three years later on 23rd May 1902 she told Mr. Macleay, *"Much of the best imaginative work of the Celtic, certainly the Gaelic peoples, is inspired by longing, and generally by the peculiar and acute longing caused by the pressure of uncongenial circumstances in a foreign atmosphere, or by absence, or by forced exile. That, and the deeper and insatiable spiritual longing that has ever characterised our race."*

These are very personal and intimate revelations of how strongly she was influenced by her deep Faery memory and ancestry and how much the link with the land is important, not just to the Faeries but to humans as well. The latter quotation is a good example of how changing the words 'Celtic' and 'Gaelic' for 'Faery' can reveal a previously unknown aspect of Faery sentiment and emotion. Note also the powerful last sentence, *"... the deeper and insatiable spiritual longing that has ever characterised our* (Faery) *race"* that tells us the Faeries also long for spiritual satisfaction; it is not just a basic human need.

In an article entitled 'From the Hebrid Isles' published in *Harper's Magazine*, December 1895, she says,

> *"One day will come when men will be sorrier for what is irrevocably lost than ever a nation mourned for a lapsed dominion. It is a bitter cruel thing that strangers must rule the hearts and brains, as well as the poor fortunes of the mountaineers and islanders. But in doing their best to thrust Celtic life, Celtic speech, Celtic thought, into the sea, they are working a sore hurt for themselves that they shall lament in the day of adversity. For we of the passing race see this thing: that in a day to come the sheep-runs shall not be in the isles and Highlands only — for we see the forests moving south, and there will be lack, then, not of deer and of sheep, but of hunters and shepherds."*

The strong sentiments and fear of loss of culture and identity expressed here show that Fiona had developed an emotional attachment with the human race, a rare thing for a Faery, and understood what a tragic loss such a passing would be to both worlds.

However, proponents of the Celtic Twilight movement of the 1890s strongly objected to the notion that the Celtic people were in decline and publicly criticised her over these comments. In response she had this to say in her essay *Iona:*

> *"A doomed and passing race. I have been taken to task for these words. But they are true, in the deep reality where they obtain. Yes, but true only in one sense, however vital that is. The Breton's eyes are slowly turning from the enchanted West, and slowly his ears are forgetting the whisper of the wind around menhir and dolmen. The Manxman has ever been the mere yeoman of the Celtic chivalry; but even his rude dialect perishes year by year. In Wales, a great tradition survives; in Ireland a supreme tradition fades through sunset-hued horizons; in Celtic Scotland, a passionate regret, a despairing love and longing, narrows yearly before a dull and incredible selfish alienism. The Celt has at last reached his horizon. There is no shore beyond. He knows it… But this apparition of a passing race is no more than the fulfilment of a glorious resurrection before our very eyes. For the genius of the Celtic race stands out now with averted torch, and the light of it is a glory before the eyes, and the flame of it is blown into the hearts of the stronger people. The Celt fades, but his spirit rises in the heart and the mind of the Anglo-Celtic peoples, with whom are the destinies of generations to come."*

This is a clear rebuff of her critics and makes it even clearer how she feels about the decline of the Celt. But, as always with Fiona's statements, there is more to this than meets the eye. The third sentence, *"But they are true, in the deep reality where they obtain"* is a subtle reference to the real decline happening in the Realm of Faery. Just as 'beauty' is a code-word for Faery so too is the word 'deep.' Fiona used the word deep many times in her writings when referring to the Realm of Faery and we shall examine a couple of important examples of this later. The direction *'where they obtain'* also points to the Realm of Faery. I should point out that the phrase *"the passing race"* is just one of many Gaelic euphemisms for the Faeries as many Gaels feel that to mention the Faeries directly by name is not a wise thing to do. The fact that she openly says *"we of the passing race"* is an admission by Fiona Macleod that she is indeed a Faery.

From time to time she also speculated on matters that we would consider to be the domain of the Christian theologian rather than the seeker after Faery. Much of this speculation was to do with the coming of the Redeemer in the form of a woman, and one who would be born in the Western Isles, Iona being the place Fiona normally named. In her essay of that name she says:

*"I believe that we are close upon a great and deep spiritual change. I believe a
new redemption is even now conceived of the Divine Spirit in the human heart,
that is itself as a woman, broken in dreams, and yet sustained in faith, patient,
long-suffering, looking towards home. I believe that though the Reign of Peace
may be yet a long way off, it is drawing near: and that Who shall save us anew
shall come divinely as a Woman. To save as Christ saved, but not as He did, to
bring with Her a sword. But whether this Divine Woman, this Mary of so many
passionate hopes and dreams, is to come through mortal birth, or as an immortal
breathing upon our souls, none can yet know.*

*Sometimes I dream of the old prophecy that Christ shall come again upon
Iona, and of that later and obscure prophecy which foretells, now as the Bride of
Christ, now as the Daughter of God, now as the Divine Spirit embodied through
mortal birth in a Woman, as once through mortal birth in a Man, the coming of
a new Presence and Power: and dream that this may be upon Iona, so that the
little Gaelic island may become as the little Syrian Bethlehem. But more wise
it is to dream, not of hallowed ground, but of the hallowed gardens of the soul
wherein She shall appear white and radiant. Or, that upon the hills, where we
are wandered, the Shepherdess shall call us home."*

She repeated this theme several times in her private correspondence and
in particular with a certain Dr. John Goodchild. For full details of this
remarkable man see my book *The Little Book of the Great Enchantment*
and also Patrick Benham's excellent book *The Avalonians*. For the
moment here is what she said to him in a letter.

*"There is a strange and obscure prophecy in the Hebrides upon which I had meant
to write a long study … I have in my mind, however, all but finally thought out
(my way of work) a spiritual study called 'The Second Coming of St Bride' which
will give utterance to this faith in a new redeeming spiritual face, — a woman
who will express the old Celtic Bride or Brigit (goddess of fire, song, music). The
first modern saintliness of woman (<u>Bride-nan-Brat</u> St Brigit of the Mantle;
<u>Muime-Chriosda</u> Christ's Foster Mother; Mary's Sister etc). The Virgin Mother
of Catholicism; Mary of Motherhood; Mary, the Goddess of the Human Soul;
Mary, Destiny; Mary, the Star-Kindler: for Destiny is but the name of the starry
light hidden in each human soul: Consolatrix: Genetrix: the immortal Sister of
Orchil, the Earth Goddess, at once Hera, Pan and Demogorgon: The Daughter
of God: The Star of Dreams; The Soul of Beauty: the Shepherd of Immortality.
In the short story called 'The Washer of the Ford'… there is a hint of this in
another way — that of the conflict between the Pagan and the early Christian*

ideals of the Mysterious Woman, whether a Celtic Fate or a Mary Bride of God: as again, in another way, in a story called 'The Woman With The Net' in the Pagan section of my forthcoming book, 'The Dominion of Dreams.'"

As well as giving little snippets of Faery lore relating to the Christ she also on occasion touched on other esoteric aspects of Christianity. For example, the following excerpt from *Iona* is quite apt today judging by the recent interest there has been in Mary Magdalene.

"A Tiree man whom I met some time ago on the boat that was taking us both to the west, told me there's a story that Mary Magdalene lies in a cave in Iona. She roamed the world with a blind man who loved her, but they had no sin. One day they came to Knoydart in Argyll. Mary Magdalene's first husband had tracked her there, and she knew that he would kill the blind man. So she bade him lie down among some swine, and she herself herded them. But her husband came and laughed at her. 'That is a fine boar you have there,' he said. Then he put a spear through the blind man. 'Now I will take your beautiful hair,' he said. He did this and went away. She wept till she died. One of Colum's monks found her, and took her to Iona, and she was buried in a cave. No one but Colum knew who she was. Colum sent away the man, because he was always mooning and lamenting. She had a great wonderful beauty to her."

This mixing of Faery tradition and unconventional Christian belief is found throughout Fiona's extensive writings. It is a subject we shall come back to time and time again.

All of these brief quotations and comments above help to reveal how Fiona thought and felt about the importance of her work, the revelation of the Faery mysteries; but they were addressed to readers who did not know that she was a Faery and that she used the physical body of William Sharp to actually put pen to paper, deal with publishers and answer her considerable correspondence. The one personality trait that does not come through from these letters and comments was her intensity, her urgency and, indeed, her relentlessness in making sure her goal was achieved. William Sharp was a physically weak man who suffered from serious chronic ill health all his life. This was exacerbated by the fact he travelled extensively, was a prolific writer under his own name and would often work for twenty-fours hours at a stretch. The excessive demands that Fiona put on him to simultaneously meet her needs while dealing with his own work as William Sharp were in great part the cause of his early death at age fifty. I have dealt with this unpleasant aspect of Fiona Macleod in *The Little Book of the Great Enchantment*. I mention it here only to demonstrate just how important it was to Fiona Macleod to make known to the human world as much as was possible during her short connection with William Sharp. An example of Fiona's refusal to acknowledge William's dangerously weak state of health is revealed in a birthday card she sent him on what would be his last birthday. It says,

"My dear Will,

Another birthday has come, and I must frankly say that apart from the loss of another year, and from what the year has brought you in love and friendship and all that makes up life, it has not been to your credit. True, you have been in America and Italy and France and Scotland and England and Germany – and so have not been long settled anywhere – and true also that for a month or two you were seriously and for a few months partially ill or 'down' – but still, after all allowances, I note not only an extraordinary indolence in effort as well as unmistakable laziness in achievement. Now, either you are growing old (in which case admit dotage, and be done with it) or else you are permitting yourself to remain weakly in futile havens of ignoble repose or fretful pseudo rest. You have much to do, or that you ought to do, yourself: and as to <u>our</u> collaboration I see no way for its continuance unless you will abrogate much of what is superfluous, curtail much that can quite well be curtailed, and generally serve me loyally as I in my turn allow for and serve <u>you</u>. Let our New Year be a very different one from the last, dear friend: and let us not only beautifully dream but <u>achieve</u> in beauty. Let the ignoble pass, and the noble remain.

Lovingly your, dear Will,
Fiona"
(Note, again, the use of the word 'beauty'.)

In *The Little Book of the Great Enchantment* I speculate on whether Fiona was aware of the debilitating effect she had on William's health. I believe she was, and whether or not she felt any regret following his death, I believe she did. William always said that if the truth about Fiona should be revealed, by which he meant that he was the author of those works, then Fiona would die. Following his death in Sicily on 12th December 1905 the secret was revealed by his widow Elizabeth, and Fiona did indeed die. For a few years after William's death Elizabeth attempted to stay in touch with him through mediums and séances. Several times during these beyond-the-grave communications William commented that Fiona "*is no more.*"

One of Fiona's American publishers was Thomas B. Mosher who only met William Sharp once, on what was to be his last visit to the United States. Mosher wrote of this meeting in his foreword to his 1907 imprint of *The Distant Country*. He finished this short piece with four lines of his own composition that imply he understood that Fiona was a sentient being in her own right. The last line shows that he also understood how Fiona drove William to an early grave by her unrelenting demands on him. This line further implies that she now feels remorse for this action and, consequently, has no desire to find 'another slave.'

> *"Death touched his wrist and took his pen,*
> *And lured him from the world of men,*
> *She mourns by that Sicilian grave,*
> *Nor roams to find another slave."*

To finish this chapter on how Fiona Macleod viewed her own writings and her self-chosen task of revealing Faery lore to Humankind I append a dedication she wrote to her friend, magical co-worker and fellow poet W.B. Yeats. From the wording she uses it is clear that she considered Yeats to be one of the few people who would understand her Faery lore. In so doing she reveals a good deal in this lengthy passage. It is my belief, after reading this dedication many times, that Fiona also considered Yeats either to be of the Faeries himself or at least to have mixed Faery and human blood. On that count she may well have been correct. The dedication is the opening section of her work *Foam of the Past*.

> *"In a small book in a greater, 'The Little Book of the Great Enchantment' in 'The Book of White Magic (or Wisdom)' ... the 'Leabhran Mhòr Gheasadaireachd' to give the Gaelic name ... it is said, 'When you have a memory out of darkness, tell to a seer, to a poet, and to a friend, that which you remember: and if the seer say, I see it — and if the poet say, I hear it — and if the friend say, I believe it: then know of a surety that your remembrance is a true remembrance.' But if our ancestral memories, or memories of the imagination, or reveries of the imagining mind wandering in a world publicly foregone yet inwardly actual, could become authentic only by a test such as this, then I fear they would indeed*

be apparent as mere foam, the froth of dream. For where is he who is at once seer and poet and friend? Well, you have the great desire, which is the threshold of vision, and vision itself you have, which is the white enchantment: your words that you compel to a new and subtle music, and the unknown airs in your mind that shepherd those words into the green glens of your imagination, would reveal you as the poet, though not one of your fellows acclaimed you, or none offered you the mistletoe bough with its old symbolism of wisdom and song: and, finally, I think I may call you friend, for we go one way, the dearer that it is narrow and little trod and leads by the whispering sedge and the wilderness, and meet sometimes on that way, and know that we seek the same Graal, and shall come upon it, beyond the fathomless hollow of green water that lies in the West as our poets say, the 'Pool' whose breath is Silence and over which hangs a bow of red flame whitening to its moonwhite core.

So you, perhaps, may say of some of these lines in 'From the Hills of Dream' and 'Foam of the Past' that they come familiarly to you in other than the sense of mere acquaintance. I think you, too, have known the dew which falls when Dalua whispers under the shadowy rowan-trees, and have heard the laughter of the Hidden Host, and known, ... not the fairie folk of later legend, ... but the perilous passage of the great Lords of Shadow, 'who tread the deeps of night.' You, too, perhaps, have feared The White Hound and The Red Shepherd: and have known that weariness, too old and deep for words, of which the aged Gaelic woman of the Island of Tiree had dim knowledge when she sang

It is the grey rock I am,
And the grey rain on the rock:
It is the grey wave ...
That grey hound.

You have heard The Rune of the Winds, the blowing of the four white winds and the three dark winds: perhaps, if you have not seen, or heard, my little Moon-Child, you remember her from long ago, and her loneliness when she sang

I have no playmate but the tide
The seaweed loves with dark brown eyes:
The night-waves have the stars for play,
For me but sighs.

For all poetry is in a sense memory: all art, indeed, is a mnemonic gathering of the innumerable and lost into the found and unique, I am sure that you, too, *have seen the rising of the Crimson Moon, and have walked secretly with Midir of the Dew and moon-crown'd Brigid and wave-footed Mânan. For you also the long way that seems brief and the short way that seems long, who can say with Dalua in 'The Immortal Hour'*

> *And if I tread the long, continuous way*
> *Within a narrow round, not thinking it long,*
> *And fare a single hour thinking it many days,*
> *I am not first or last of the Immortal Clan*
> *For whom the long ways of the world are brief*
> *And the short ways heavy with unimagined time.*

I have listened so long to the music of the three harpers of Fraech, that what I most love now in the cadence and inward breath of song is that which comes across the thorn. You remember them, the three sons of Boinn of the Sidhe, that fair queen: the three harpers of Fraech in the old tale of the 'Tain Bo Fraich' ... who had for bard names Tear-Bringer, Smile-Bringer, and Sleep-Bringer: and how it was from the music of Uaithne, the self-playing harp of the Everlasting One, that these three were named. And I, too, like Befinn, sister of Boinn, am spell-bound in that vision of sorrowful beauty ... of beauty that comes secretly out of darkness and greyness and the sighing of wind, as the dew upon the grass and the reed by pale water: and is, for so brief a while: and, as the dew is gathered again swiftly and in silence, is become already a dream, a lost air remembered, a beautiful thing that might have been. For that is what is hidden in the lament of the shennachies of old, when they sang of the loveliness of Befinn fading, like a leaf of May at the cold fires of Samhain, before the great flame of beauty of her son Fraech, 'most beautiful of the men of Erin and Albin' ... because of what she saw in that exceeding beauty, like the blue dusk at the heart of flame. 'Beautiful beyond all beauty of youth, he was: but he has not long lived.' That is the burden of the song. And what is this deep undertide of longing for that which is beyond wavering reach, for that which is covered up in the secrecies of things immortal, but the longing of Finnavar, daughter of bright Oilill and dark-browed Maeve, for Fraech, the Son of Beauty, though she had never seen him, and loved only by hearsay, and because of the white passion in her heart, and because that inappeasable desire was more great to her than the things of life? Alas, what sorrowful truth lies in that dark saying of Boinn of the Sidhe ... 'Men shall die who have an ear for harmonies.'

So that, to you, for one, these poems, however rude in form they may sometimes be, will come with that remembrance of the imagination which is the incalculable air of the otherworld of poetry. As you know, most of them have their place in tales of mine coloured with the colour of a lost day and of a beauty that is legend: and must suffer by severance from their context, as pluckt pine-branches lose, if not their native savour, at least the light and gloom of their forest-company and the smooth hand of the wind. The sound and colour of a barbarous day may well vanish in the recalling of those broken strains... at their best dimly caught even when, for example, 'The Death Dance' be read in its due place in 'The Laughter of the Queen,' apart from which it is perhaps like an air born a thousand years ago on a Gaelic minstrel's clarsach and played anew today with curious artifice on a many noted instrument. One or two at least of these threnodies and chants will have for you the familiar cadence of thought as well as of the familiar fall of words, for they are but adaptations of what long ago were chanted to rude harps made of applewood and yew. The songs of the Swan-Children of Lir have been sung by many poets: Deirdre's Lament on leaving Scotland, as she and Naoise crossed the Irish Sea, has been a music in every generation of the Gael: and I do no more than remember, and repeat, with an accent of atmosphere or thought or words, which, perhaps, just reveals the difference between paraphrase and metaphrase. Like Deirdre, we, too, look often yearningly to a land from which we were exiled in time, but inhabit in dream and longing, saying with her

> *Glen of the Roes, Glen of the Roes,*
> *In thee I have dreamed to the full my happy dream:*
> *O that where the shallow bickering Ruel flows*
> *I might hear again, o'er its flashing gleam,*
> *The cuckoos calling by the murmuring stream.*

Take time to study this long passage. It will reveal much.

Chapter Three

THE FAERY TRADITION

How beautiful they are,
The lordly ones
Who dwell in the hills,
In the hollow hills.

THERE ARE SEVERAL basic aspects of the Faery tradition that bear close resemblance to some human magical systems, but the subtle differences between them are important and must be identified and understood before the system will reveal of its fullest. This may be more challenging for the experienced magician than for the newcomer but that very challenge can be turned into a valuable learning experience. To some readers what follows may go against the grain of cherished beliefs or deeply ingrained practices and rituals but I must stress that none of this requires the letting-go of any current magical practice or system, nor does it require an exclusive dedication to the Faery tradition. The only important point that must constantly be adhered to is not to mix traditions. For example, should you be performing a traditional Wiccan seasonal festival then keep it Wiccan – do not attempt to add in a little bit of Faery. Similarly if you are practicing one of the several branches of what has come to be known as the Western Mystery Tradition then by all means occasionally take a foray into the Realm of Faery but leave your Western Mystery Tradition accoutrements and beliefs in the Lodge, do not take them with you.

A good example of how the Faery-based magical system has become entangled with a human-based magical system is that of the Celtic tradition. There are some solid historical and literary reasons why these two traditions were at one time closely linked but they have always been sufficiently separate and independent to make them distinct from each other. Today the lines have been crossed in both directions and aspects of one have now become accepted canon in the other. This confusion is not helped when reading the works of Fiona Macleod as she frequently seems to mix the two together willy-nilly. However, a closer examination of what she is actually saying, and especially a closer look at her interpretation of individual words, starts to make the differences clear. I have deliberately chosen throughout this book examples of her works that give valuable Faery lore that is easily mistaken for Celtic lore. At such points in the text I give arguments as to why I believe her point at issue is more Faery than it is Celtic. Having said that, knowledge of the Celtic magical system is not a bad thing to have and can be helpful when learning the Faery tradition.

The first thing to point out from a spiritual point of view is that the Faery tradition is not a religious system. Although the Faeries have their own pantheon of gods and goddesses, discussed later, they are not worshipped in any manner that we would understand, nor are they regarded in any way as being superior or more powerful in a religious or spiritual sense than either Faeries or humans. Therefore the Faery tradition should not interfere or conflict with any existing religious belief or practice that the reader may already follow.

A good example of two traditions existing side by side is the Faery tradition and the early Celtic Christian church. It has always seemed to me that many of the early Celtic Christian saints come across as being much more Faery than they do human or Christian. With this in mind it is interesting to note how often Fiona Macleod wrote stories about St. Columba of Iona and manages to mention him many times in stories and essays, even ones that do not deal directly with the saint. She clearly felt comfortable retelling some of the old tales of this fiery 6th century Irish cleric as well as introducing us to some that had never previously been seen, at least in the human world. By so doing she was pointing out that much can be gleaned regarding Faery lore by studying the life and works of St. Columba.

I stress elsewhere in this book that there can be some dangers connected with the Faery Tradition but that they can be easily recognised and dealt with before they become a problem. In *The Little Book of the Great Enchantment* I include an entire appendix on Fiona's play *The Immortal Hour* and how Netta Fornario, a real human being who was obsessed with this play, ignored the warning signs that she was getting deeper into the Faery realm than was safe. Her dead body was found on the Isle of Iona in very strange circumstances.

The cause of Netta's strange death and curious activities prior to her disappearance on Iona stem from her obsession with the writings of Fiona Macleod. Part of her motivation almost certainly stemmed from a tale in Fiona's essay *Iona,* telling how when she was a child living on the island she went to visit a friend, Elsie, whom she had not seen for some time. When she got to the house her friend's mother said that Elsie was gone and had not been seen for some time. Fiona was puzzled, as she knew that if Elsie had left by the small ferry to Mull she would certainly have heard of it. Elsie's mother then told Fiona that her daughter had been in communication with the spirits of the old monks from Columba's time and they were hostile to her. She only felt safe on one part of the island, a place where the spirits of the monks could not go. Elsie's mother explained, *"The monks are still the strongest here... That is, except over by Staonaig. Up between Sgeur Iolaire and Cnoc Druidean there's a path that no monk can go. There, in the old days, they burned a woman. She was not a woman but they thought she was. She was one of the Sorrows of the Sheen, (Faeries) ... It's ill to any that brings harm to 'them'. That's why the monks are not strong over by Staonaig way."*

Netta Fornario was familiar with the essay *Iona,* and the places that are mentioned in this little tale would also have been familiar to her. They still bear the same names today. Loch Staonaig (the curved lake) is the name of the small freshwater loch at the south end of the island, Sgeur Iolaire (the Point of the Eagle) is now called Sròn Iolaire (the Nose of the Eagle) and lies north of Loch Staonaig, with Cnoc na Druidean (Hill of the Starlings) a very short way further north. Between them is the path that Fiona's friend said the monks could not travel on. This is where Netta Fornario's body was found. Before she died she had told her landlady on the island that she had a "terrible case of healing" underway. Was this magical work actually an attempt by her to bring peace to the Faery woman that was so badly treated there, or, perhaps, was she trying to bring healing and closure to the monks who committed the foul deed in the first place? We shall never know. Whatever she was attempting it brought about her death. This is obviously an extreme example but it is one from recent factual history and clearly illustrates how information can be gleaned from the writings of Fiona Macleod but that it is imperative to understand what that information is and how to use it safely.

But to return to the magical aspect of Faery – there are some fundamental and important differences between the Faery magical system and the Western Mystery Tradition and Wiccan magical systems that need to be understood. The basis of almost all ceremonies and rituals within both the Western Mystery Tradition and Wiccan tradition is the use of the Four Elements – Earth, Water, Fire and Air – and the Four Directions (or Quarters) – North, South, East and West. These are an integral part in one way or another of almost every magical ceremony and ritual, and they form the solid grounding of these physical world-based traditions. The Golden Dawn system of magic makes much use of the Four Directions and Four Elements and attributes many other layers of fours to these, including the Four Archangels, the Four Magical Tools (or Weapons) and so forth. William Sharp's friend and magical collaborator, William Butler Yeats, Irish poet, mystic and statesman, started his own secret magical order while still a member of the Golden Dawn. This was the Celtic Mystical Order and its main focus was in retrieving knowledge concerning the Four Treasures of the Tuatha De Danann: the Sword of Nuada, the Spear of Lugh, the Cauldron of the Dagda and the Lia Fáil or Stone of Destiny.

These 'fours' are fundamental to many magical systems and are of great magical value, but because they are based on physical elements and spatial directions of the human world they have little relevance in the non-human world of Faery where such things do not exist, at least as we know them. When working within the Faery tradition, the physical building blocks of this world – the Four Elements, and the coordinates of physical space, the Four Directions – are not as necessary and are not as symbolically powerful in a world that is not solid and where movement is not limited to spatial directions. Having said that, you will see in Chapter Nine, where I discuss the Four Cities, that Fiona does attribute a direction and an Element to each of these four Faery locations; we can look at this apparent anomaly more closely in that chapter. For the time being just keep in mind that for most Faery magical workings the Four Directions and the four physical Elements are superfluous, and do not bring any energy or power to the working in hand.

They do have an oblique value, however, in that many magicians may well feel uncomfortable performing any sort of magical work when these basics have been omitted. Should you feel that way then by all means include the Opening of the Quarters and the Invocation of the Elements if it will put you into a less tense frame of mind. Their inclusion will not have a disruptive or negative effect on the working, so they are safe to include from that point of view, but if including them has a beneficial calming effect on the individual magician then that in itself makes them worthwhile. I would however strongly encourage the sincere and earnest seekers after Faery to cut them out altogether if at all possible. By being prepared to open up and experiment, you will gain much more, and much more quickly. As Fiona Macleod said, what you bring to the enchantment is more important than what you expect to take away from it.

Whether you choose to retain the Four Elements and Four Directions or not, there are several other groups of four that *are* relevant and to which we must pay heed. Fiona used these fours frequently in her writings, and their importance can easily be overlooked by a mind that is trained to pay attention only to Elements and Directions. Some examples of other Faery fours are the Four Keys, Four Cities, Four Coloured Winds, and the more subtle but still important motif of events within a story repeating four times but on different levels. More will be said on all of these fours throughout this book.

Returning for a moment to the fours of the human world, it is worth considering that it is only since the 1970s that the magical Opening of the Four Directions and the use of pathworkings (inner journeys, guided meditations, visualisations or whatever you wish to call them) have become common knowledge and magical practice outside the walls of the magical lodge. Prior to then they were techniques only to be found in closed occult groups and were not usually made public. Nowadays though it seems it has become obligatory to open the Four Directions and do a visualisation at almost every public talk, presentation, workshop etc no matter what the subject of the talk is and without regard to the magical skill, or otherwise, of the members of the public present. I would argue that over the past forty or so years these techniques have become so overused that they are now meaningless and virtually useless. We have sucked the battery dry. The Opening of the Four Directions and the use of pathworkings in a specific ritual within a private lodge or coven are still valid but the common situation today of large, public events utilizing these techniques has weakened their power to the point that it is almost nil. The time has come for a radical, but necessary, change in what we accept as normal magical practice. The Faery tradition offers just such an opportunity.

To this end it is important to know how to respectfully and successfully contact Faeries and how to travel safely and with clear intention in their realm. To achieve such success it is necessary to lay aside preconceived ideas and notions as to the nature of Faeries and the Realm of Faery: they are rarely what the newcomer expects. It is also necessary to lay aside preconceived ideas and notions as to what will happen once access has been gained to this non-physical realm.

Is this not the way we should go about travelling and making contact in this world? When I phone my friend I do not have a preconceived notion of exactly when he will answer, what mood he will be in or how the exact word-for-word exchange of our conversation will flow. I call, wait, and, once he answers, take it as it comes. When I visit a foreign country I do not presume to know in exact detail how every local person I encounter will behave, how I will be treated, where we shall all go and how it will all turn out in the end. I will certainly have read up in travel books some of the basic information I will need to avoid dangerous or unintentionally disrespectful situations. But I do not arrive there with my head crammed full of detailed ideas of exactly how the next few weeks, days or even hours will pass. So too with Faery. Any such detailed anticipations are at best arrogant and at worst nothing more than a mental block prohibiting full, clear and conscious communication to take place. It is instructive to note that even William Sharp, who worked so closely with the Faery Fiona Macleod, never asked her directly what she was doing or what her intentions were. He watched, listened, paid attention and acted upon her needs and requirements as they arose. This approach worked very well for both parties and it should be a good starting point for anyone wishing to make meaningful Faery communication.

The three most common methods used by Faery to communicate with humans are:

1) direct Inner communication, whether audibly, visually or both;
2) the subtle insertion by a Faery contact of ideas, hunches and hints into the conscious human mind during ritual and visualisation;
3) synchronicity in making what you need available when you need it during your day-to-day routine.

The first of these is not usually achieved to any great degree until the student has spent some time practising Realm of Faery travelling and contact, unless he or she is already particularly psychic. The eventual success of this approach is usually high but it is totally dependent on the whim of the Faery contact, not on the skill of the would-be magician. To use the analogy of the phone call again – sometimes when I call my friend he is too busy to speak with me at any length and I must try again later. So too with Faery.

The second communication method: ideas, hunches and hints that suddenly pop into your mind, apparently from nowhere and apparently without cause, probably happens more than most magicians realise. Once you decide to take upon yourself the long-term commitment of communicating with the Faeries you must be constantly vigilant and receptive to such intuitive nudging. Communication does not necessarily only happen when you have set aside some time and are deep in visualization. Your mind is often most receptive when it is least cluttered with magical intentions and actions. If you are peeling the potatoes for dinner and an idea pops into your thoughts regarding some earlier Faery communication then pay attention to it. Should you be half-asleep and you suddenly have a strong urge to read or reread some book or other then take note of that and do so the next day. Pay particular attention to such strong urges and thoughts that at first may seem unconnected to any Faery work you have been doing. Perhaps you have been heading too far down the wrong track but were unable to see this. When you are not thinking on it is the best time for your Faery communicator to drop that idea into your uncluttered thoughts. It takes time to recognise when such unexpected ideas are indeed real communications and when they are no more than the daydreaming of a relaxed mind. Learn to trust your intuition in these matters, not your logical mind.

The third communication method is the rarest but often the one with the most impact when it happens. The life of William Sharp was full of such astonishing moments of synchronicity, and instances of what was needed magically and in the day-to-day world becoming available just when it was needed most. Many magicians will find this happening only once or twice during any set programme of Faery magical study, but when it does it is unmistakable and results in a powerful reinforcement of the belief in the validity of successful human and Faery communication. While researching and writing *The Little Book of the Great Enchantment* I personally had so many such 'synchronicities' that I was compelled to include them in the book. Now, as I write this current book, I am finding that once again some surprising coincidences are happening to me. For example, when I had finished writing Chapter Ten, "Joy and Sorrow", I received an email from an acquaintance who knew nothing of what I was writing at that time. She concluded her message with these words, "*Worry does not empty today of its sorrow, it empties today of its joy and strength.*" I took this synchronistic event to mean I was on the right track.

There will be times when despite your best efforts your Faery contact may not want to communicate with you. This is a situation that will arise from time to time and the student needs to know how to handle and cope with it. A common reaction is that the magician believes he or she has done something wrong technically or has inadvertently caused some offence to the Faery contact, and that the contact has decided to move elsewhere. This is very unlikely to be the case. Remember that the Faeries need to work just as hard to contact us as we do to contact them and they will not storm off in a huff any more than you should. But, like my friend who sometimes just decides not to answer his phone, your Faery contact may have other things on her/his plate at the time you wish to speak with her/him. If that should be the case then try 'calling back' later. It is no big deal.

However the exact opposite of this scenario can cause problems. One situation that may arise when things are going particularly well is that your Faery ally may become a little bit too enthusiastic and you may find you are being pushed to your limit as far as demands on your time and accessibility are concerned. On occasion you may need to set boundaries. This is important. The energy level of the Faeries is far higher than that of most humans and, just as in any other task or daily routine, it is necessary to take a break every now and then in order to relax, refresh and start anew with fresh vigour and enthusiasm. To make yourself available 24/7 for every whim and idea that your Faery contact may have is definitely not a good idea for either of you. A look at the day-to-day life of William Sharp should serve as a salutary example of what happens when boundaries are not set. This was indeed an extreme case but nonetheless you must recognise your own limits and stamina and when they have been reached you must take a break.

Once you have both found a mutually acceptable level of working then another situation calling for some caution and self-assertion may arise. As your Faery contact becomes more confident in you and your abilities you may well find that he or she raises topics that you do not understand or brings up issues that seem pointless or irrelevant. This is quite natural as Faery needs are different from human need – which of course means that you too may well be bringing up topics and issues with her/him that are important to you but that make no sense to her/him. However if you find yourself spending an inordinate amount of time on something that you just cannot understand, or which seems to demand an excessive amount of time and energy on your part for little, if any, return, then it is acceptable to say politely but clearly, "No. I am not doing it." And, believe me, if you make excessive demands on your Faery contact that is exactly what he/she will say to you! This is as crucial for your own physical and emotional health as is taking a break every now and then.

Chapter Four

COMMENTS ON FAERIES
IN GENERAL

It is a strange thing: that a nation can hold within itself an ancient race, standing for the lost, beautiful, mysterious ancient world, can see it fading through its dim twilight, without heed to preserve that which might yet be preserved, without interest even in that which once gone cannot come again.

MOST OF THE references Fiona made to Faeries in her writings were oblique, confused with references to Celtic and Gaelic and rarely of a direct nature. However there were a few occasions when she did specifically comment on Faeries and the Realm of Faery. We shall look at those in a moment, but before Fiona arrived on the scene in 1893, and before William Sharp ever made note or comment on Faeries, there was a small but significant incident from William's early childhood that in many ways laid the groundwork for the arrival of Fiona decades later. He would later recall this incident thus.

"For I, too, have my dream, my memory of one whom as a child I called Star-Eyes and whom later I called 'Baumorair-na-Mara', The Lady of the Sea, and whom at least I knew to be none other than the woman who is in the heart of Women. I was not more than seven when, one day, by a well near a sea loch in Argyll, just as I was stooping to drink, my glancing eyes lit on a tall woman standing amongst a mist of wild hyacinths under three great sycamores. I stood, looking, as a fawn looks, wide-eyed, unafraid. She did not speak, but she smiled and because of the love and beauty in her eyes I ran to her. She stooped and

52

lifted blueness out of the flowers, as one might lift foam out of a pool, and I thought she threw it over me. When I was found lying among the hyacinths dazed, and, as was thought, ill, I asked eagerly after the lady in white and with hair all shiny gold like buttercups, but when I found I was laughed at or at least, when I passionately persisted, was told I was sun dazed and had been dreaming, I said no more — but I did not forget."

The importance of this is lost unless we understand that the Victorian attitude to Faeries was one of fear and avoidance. It was a well-known fact that Faery women often stole human children and raised them as their own in the Faery Realm. So when the seven-year-old William gleefully recounted his close encounter of the Faery kind it no doubt brought a pang of fear to his parents, hopefully to be quickly followed by a sense of relief that their beloved son had survived the attempted kidnapping. He, though, remembered the incident all his life and perhaps felt a little regret that an adventure into the Realm of Faery had been denied. The name he gave to the Faery woman is interesting: 'Baumorair-na-Mara', The Lady of the Sea. Fiona Macleod would later come to make her presence known following an incident centred around a deep lake, and many of her tales concern the sea, fishermen, island life, drowning, lakes, streams and other watery connections. But note that he says of this Faery woman, *"as a child I called* (her) *Star-Eyes and ... later I called* (her) *'Baumorair-na-Mara', The Lady of the Sea."* So in his childhood innocence he gave her a name that reflected her appearance, specifically her beautiful eyes, but later – after Fiona arrived? – he connected her with the sea. It is perfectly possible that this childhood Faery was in fact Fiona.

The act that the Lady of the Sea performed, throwing the blueness of the hyacinths over him, was nothing less than a Faery baptism. It was this early initiation into the Realm of Faery that made William Sharp such a suitable vehicle for Fiona Macleod to work through in later life. Note that he described her location very specifically as being "under three great sycamores". The number three is always significant in these matters, but more importantly, in early and medieval Faery lore, and in particular the Faery lore scattered throughout the Arthurian legends, sycamores are symbolic of the entry point to the Realm of Faery. So this little childhood vignette that William Sharp cherished all his life really 'set the scene' for the later corpus of Faery lore revealed by the Faery writer Fiona Macleod.

Fiona too recounted a personal story of the Faeries from her childhood. In her essay *Iona* she said:

"As a child I had some wise as well as foolish instruction concerning the nations of Faerie. If, in common with nearly all happy children, I was brought up in intimate, even in circumstantial, knowledge of 'the fairies'... I was told also of the Sidhe, often so rashly and ignorantly alluded to as the fairies in the sense of a pretty, diminutive, harmless, natural folk; and by my nurse Barabal instructed in some of the ways, spells, influences, and even appearances of these powerful and mysterious clans.

I do not think, unless as a very young child, I ever confused them. I recollect well my pleasure at a sign of gratitude... I was fond of making little reed flutes, but once... I lost the only one I had. That night I put aside a small portion of my supper... and remember also the sacrifice of a gooseberry of noble proportions... Next morning when I ran out... I saw by the emptied saucer my little reed flute! Here was proof positive! I was so grateful for that fairy's gratitude, that when dusk came again I not only left a larger supper-dole than usual, but, decked with white fox-glove bells... sat drenched in dew and played my little reed. Any moment (I was sure) a small green fellow would appear, [but] with wild indignation I found myself snatched from the grass [by nurse Barabal], and my ears dinned with reproaches about the dew... ah, there are souls that know nothing of fairies...!

But the Sidhe are a very different people from the small clans of the earth's delight."

This little vignette makes it very clear that the Sidhe are not to be confused with the fairies, and that amongst both of these races there are many different clans, or groups. It may well be asked how did the child Fiona Macleod gain such certainty in these matters? The answer is that she was speaking with the knowledge of an insider. She continued this theme by quoting from one of her intended but never published books (of which there were many) called *The Chronicles of the Sidhe*. Like several of the other books she mentioned and quoted from, this is a book that exists only in the Realm of Faery but she clearly had had plans to publish it in physical form in our world. This never happened, but fortunately she did quote from it extensively within her *Iona* essay. This is a long but important passage so for ease of reference we shall examine it in several sections.

The opening paragraphs say:

"It is commonly said that the People of the Sidhe dwell within hills, or in the underworld. In some of the isles their home, now, is spoken of as Tir-na-Thonn, the Land of the Wave, or Tir-fo-Tuinn, the Land under the Sea.

But from a friend, an islander of Iona, I have learned many things; among them, that the Shee no longer dwell within the inland hills, and that though many of them inhabit the lonelier isles of the west, and in particular The Seven Hunters, their kingdom is in the North.

Some say it is among the pathless mountains of Iceland. But my friend spoke to an Iceland man, and he said he had never seen them. There were Secret People there, but not the Gaelic Sidhe.

Their Kingdom is in the North, under the 'Fir-Chlisneach,' the Dancing Men, as the Hebrideans call the polar aurora. They are always young there. Their bodies are white as the wild swan, their hair yellow as honey, their eyes blue as ice. Their feet leave no mark on the snow. The women are white as milk, with eyes like sloes, and lips like red rowans. They fight with shadows, and are glad; but the shadows are not shadows to them. The Shee slay great numbers at the full moon, but never hunt on moonless nights, or at the rising of the moon, or when the dew is falling. Their lances are made of reeds that glitter like shafts of ice, and it is ill for a mortal to find one of these lances, for it is tipped with the salt of a wave that no living thing has touched, neither the wailing mew nor the finned 'sgadan' [Gaelic — herring] nor his tribe, nor the narwhal. There are no men of the human clans there, and no shores, and the tides are forbidden."

It is interesting to note that Fiona included the small whale known as the narwhal in this discussion. Narwhals are only found in the Arctic region and as we shall see this region is deeply connected with the Realm of Faery. Their unique, spiralling horn (which is actually an elongated tooth) was long believed to be the horn of the fabulous unicorn. And unicorns have become connected with the Faeries in popular folklore.

Note that this first excerpt starts by repeating the commonly accepted wisdom that the Faeries live in hollow hills. However Fiona then goes on to reveal that they also live in a land that is under the waves and the sea. As commented above with regard to William Sharp's own Faery encounter, the sea is a place that Fiona dealt with frequently throughout her writings. For example in the essay entitled *The Gaelic Heart*, which forms part of *The Winged Destiny*, she says:

"I have heard often in effect, 'This is no deep heart that in one hour weeps and in the next laughs.' But I know a deeper heart that in one hour weeps and in the

next laughs, so deep that light dies away within it, and silence and the beginning and the end are one: the heart of the sea."

She was clearly trying to point out that it is time we stopped looking only to the hollow hills for the Faeries, we should also look under the waves. The Arthurian tradition is full of such pointers as well, especially the frequent occurrence of the unnamed 'Lake,' as in The Lady of the Lake, Sir Lancelot du Lac, and the esoteric teaching that the young Arthur was groomed for kingship by Merlin under the waters of this same lake. It was from the lake that the fantastic sword Excalibur was drawn and eventually returned. Take note of these references to the sea, rivers and lakes, they are important.

But back to *The Chronicles of the Sidhe*. Fiona then goes on to make quite a startling new revelation. *"But from a friend, an islander of Iona, I have learned… that the Shee no longer dwell within the inland hills, and that though many of them inhabit the lonelier isles of the west… their kingdom is in the North… under the 'Fir-Chlisneach,' the Dancing Men, as the Hebrideans call the polar aurora."* First it needs to be pointed out that the tiny Inner Hebridean island of Iona, in Scotland, is considered to be a very 'thin' place; a place where the veil between this world and the Faery Realm is so thin that at times you feel like you can reach through and touch the other side. When she speaks of a friend who was an islander of Iona she is referring obliquely to a fellow Faery. This Faery-in-the-know tells Fiona that the Faeries have abandoned their ancient and traditional subterranean homes and have all but completely left Scotland and now live high in the Arctic regions under the Aurora Borealis. (See also the quotation below from *The Four Winds of Eirinn* that repeats this assertion that the Faeries have left their traditional homes.) This raises many questions and contains a lot of links to other lore and beliefs that we must examine.

The question that comes to mind is why remove to the Arctic? Fiona mentions the Arctic, Iceland, icebergs etc, in several places throughout her writings, and this in itself tells us to pay attention to these locations. For example, in a short essay on her old mentor Seumas Macleod she says, *"I remember asking him once … 'And Mânan … does he live?' 'Ay, for sure. He was here before Christ came. He will see the end of all endings. They say he sleeps in the hollows of great oceans, and sits on mountain-bergs of ice at the Pole, chanting an old ancient chant.'"*

During William Sharp's short life the Arctic was very much in the news and in the public mind and imagination. The search for the elusive

Northwest Passage had taken many lives, had inspired many acts of heroism and bravery (as well as some of astonishing stupidity) and was still on-going. The frozen Polar Regions were uncharted, unmapped and open to wild speculation as to what would be found there. It was a mysterious and distant place to most people – what better location for the mysterious and distant Faeries? Also if we look at things in reverse as it were, there are many legends that state the Faeries had originally come to our world from the far North in the first place. For example, the old Gaelic legend to be found in Scotland and Ireland of the coming to this world of the Tuatha De Danann, synonymous with the Faeries, says, *"The Tuatha De Danann were in the far Northern Isles of the world studying occult lore and sorcery ... in four cities Falias, Gorias, Murias and Findias."* The information being given out in *The Chronicles of the Sidhe* is therefore telling us that the Faeries were simply returning to their own homelands. This begs the question, what caused the Faeries to abandon their ancient hollow hill homes in the Celtic countries and relocate so far away? We shall come back to that in a moment.

The deeper meaning behind this Otherworldly exodus though has little to do with specific physical locations at all despite the clear references to Iona, Hebridean Isles, Iceland and the Arctic. The Realm of Faery is essentially located everywhere. It is above, within and below the physical world that we inhabit. Not being a physical place it has no one specific physical location. What this short revelation could be saying allegorically is that the Faeries decided to distance themselves from further human contact. It is their equivalent of turning their backs on us. They no longer wish to speak to us.

The fact that they wish to distance themselves from human contact is reflected in the tale above where it says, *"the Shee no longer dwell within the inland hills, and ... many of them inhabit the lonelier isles of the west ..."* In other words, the few places where people do not live. This is highlighted again later in the narrative when we are told, *"There are no men of the human clans there, and no shores, and the tides are forbidden."* By using the imagery of being in the remote and uncharted Polar Regions, Fiona's islander friend from Iona is actually saying, *"We are still here but you are going to have to work harder to contact us. We are not prepared to come to you so openly any more. You must make the voyage to us."* This is summed up in the last sentence of this passage from *The Chronicles of the Sidhe* (given later) that says, *"It must be hard to find that glen at the heart of the green diamond that is the world; but, when found, harder to return by the way one came."*

In other words it is still possible to find the Faery Realm, although it takes greater effort, and if successful the seeker will be forever changed by the experience, or, as the Chronicle cryptically puts it, will find it *"harder to return by the way one came."* It is harder because the traveller is a changed person. Old skills and abilities will not necessarily help on the return journey.

Note the interesting comment that *"There are no ... shores, and the tides are forbidden"* in this new Faery homeland. As explained above, this place is not a physical place, so there would be no shores or tides there anyway – so why make this comment? The insertion of this little piece of information is more revealing than it seems. Shores and beaches crop up frequently in Celtic and Faery stories and legends. Apart from making the important link with the sea, discussed earlier, these locations are what can best be called 'in-between' places. A beach or shoreline is neither dry and solid ground nor is it free flowing water. It is in-between these two specific states, it partakes of the nature of both of them. Such in-between places in our world are often entryways to the Realm of Faery, hence the reason they crop up so often in folk-tales, stories and legends. The tides are mentioned because they continue the theme of shores, but tides are also physical-world manifestations of the regular passage of time. We can calculate ahead with certainty and accuracy the next occurrence of high and low tides in this world because of their regular ebb and flow. It is interesting to note the use of the word 'forbidden' in connection with the lack of tides. This implies they are theoretically possible but they have been forbidden by the will of the Faeries.

In the Faery Realm, however, the regular flow of time simply does not exist as we know it. This is shown over and over again by the number of stories that exist involving people thinking they have only been in the Realm of Faery for a short period of time when in our world centuries have passed, or vice versa. This theme is played out in the latter part of this passage (given below) when Oran returns to Iona after being away for more than three centuries, but the monks think he has only been missing for one night. The point behind this statement though, that the new location of the Faeries has neither shores nor tides, is a cryptic way of saying the old entry points to Faery have been closed and that the Faeries now no longer accept the physical-world illusion of the regular passing of time as being relevant to their world. In short, the human world has been well and truly locked out. Which brings us back to the question posed above – what has caused the Faeries to abandon their old homes and break contact with humans?

There are many possible answers to this and it has been the subject of much debate for a long time, as hints of this split have been filtering through to us since the days of William Sharp and Fiona Macleod. The modern way of thinking has it that the Faeries, who are often seen either as Nature spirits or as being very close to Nature spirits, are upset by modern humankind's destruction of the environment and total disregard for the needs and requirements of all the other living species on the planet. This theme is stated quite specifically in Fiona's short story *Cuilidh Mhoire* (the Treasury of Mary), to be found in the collection called *The Winged Destiny*. In this tale Fiona talks about various states of being. With regard to the Realm of Faery she says, *"And what the people were then, in the many, they still are in the few; though now for the most part only where the Great Disenchantment has not yet wholly usurped the fading dominion of the Great Enchantment."* The terms Great Enchantment and Great Disenchantment refer to the Realm of Faery and the human world respectively. Here she clearly states that the human world is fast pushing the Realm of Faery further and further away and this may be the reason for the departure of the Faeries.

Another common argument put forward to explain why the Faeries have decided to withdraw is because of the predominance in our world of 'church-based' religions in favour of the older emphasis on personal human spiritual development obtained through a symbiotic relationship with the Green World. Whereas it is perfectly possible to maintain a strong belief in and adherence to a formal religion without the need to give up a close and deep personal contact with Nature and the Faeries, as displayed over and over again in Fiona's writings and in Alexander Carmichael's wonderful collection of Gaelic sayings, spells, charms and runes *Carmina Gadelica*, many followers of the church's teachings have forgotten their old beliefs and practices and moved away from the open, green spaces of the natural world to the enclosing walls of a church, synagogue, mosque or other human built structure designed to contain and shut out. But note that this does not mean the Faeries are anti-Christian, or anti-Semitic or anti any human religion. Such belief systems mean little to them.

It has also been suggested, perhaps not unwisely, that the powerful and proud Faeries of old have been so overshadowed in the popular mind by the miniature, winged and tinselled Tinker Bells of modern times that they have left us to these cartoon beings in disgust. Considering that it is only in the last hundred years or so that the popular attitude to Faeries has changed from one of fear and avoidance to one of enjoying the pretty little playthings, and that it was at exactly this same time the original Tinker Bell was introduced to the theatre-going public, this could be the case. If we are more drawn to the fragile, star-spangled and rainbow-hued sprites of the artist's imagination than we are to the real, powerful and proud Faeries of old then these same proud people are entitled to leave us to our illusions and fantasies.

Any of the above possible reasons why the Faeries have withdrawn could be true but I would argue that the sentiments all of these possible reasons express reflect more of the way humans emotionally view the world than the way Faeries do. Faeries do not necessarily share the same emotions, values or concerns that we do. We need to look deeper into the question than this and attempt to see things from the Faery perspective, not from a point of view that we are imposing on them. The best place to look for such clues is in the writings of Fiona Macleod and also in examining how Fiona lived her life in combination with that of William Sharp.

Throughout their relationship together Fiona Macleod showed very little emotional or personal concern for the health of William Sharp, and it could be argued that in so doing, she drove him relentlessly to an early grave. Anyone who wishes to work on any serious magical or spiritual level with the Faeries has to accept the fact that they are a different order of being with different priorities, different needs and different expectations. There are times when our two worlds meet, and there are times when the circumstances in one are such that the assistance of the other is required. Despite all this talk of the Faeries withdrawing from human contact, there are still rare occasions when an individual Faery, such as Fiona Macleod, takes it upon his or her self to approach us and attempt to explain the Faery lore to humankind. The many problems that Fiona Macleod had over the years she worked with William Sharp only serve to show that this was not an easy objective to achieve and this clearly emphasises what was said above regarding the differences between human and Faery. Towards the end of William Sharp's life Fiona was just starting to understand human emotions, needs and expectations and was successfully putting across her knowledge in a manner that she had struggled to achieve in her earlier writings.

I believe that throughout time there have been other Faeries with a like-mind who also wished to work magically and spiritually with humankind; Fiona Macleod was certainly not alone. But the bulk of the dwellers in the Realm of Faery are not the slightest bit interested in such ambitions and are pleased to remain hidden in the hollow hills and in the polar regions. And is this not the case with the vast majority of humans who have no interest at all in any serious attempt at communicating with a Faery, spirit or Otherworld being of any nature, and are content to turn their back on the whole subject? At least this is one commonality to be found between the bulk of Faeries and the bulk of humankind!

After introducing the concept that the Faeries have withdrawn or are withdrawing, *The Chronicles of the Sidhe* abruptly changes subject and goes on to say:

"Long ago one of the monks of Columba sailed there (the Arctic). *He sailed for thrice seven days until he lost the rocks of the north; and for thrice thirty days, till Iceland in the south was like a small bluebell in a great grey plain; and for thrice three years among bergs. For the first three years the finned things of the sea brought him food; for the second three years he knew the kindness of the creatures of the air; and in the last three years angels fed him. He lived among the Sidhe for three hundred years. When he came back to Iona, he was asked where he had been all that long night since evensong to matins. The monks had sought him everywhere, and at dawn had found him lying in the hollow of the long wave that washes Iona in the north. He laughed at that, and said he had been on the tops of the billows for nine years and three months and twenty-one days, and for three hundred years had lived among a deathless people. He had drunk sweet ale every day, and every day had known love among flowers and green bushes, and at dusk had sung old beautiful forgotten songs, and with star-flame had lit strange fires, and at the full of the moon had gone forth laughing to slay. It was heaven, there, under the Lights of the North. When he was asked how that people might be known, he said that away from there they had a cold, cold hand, a cold, still voice, and cold ice-blue eyes. They had four cities at the four ends of the green diamond that is the world. That in the north was made of earth; that in the east, of air; that in the south, of fire; that in the west, of water. In the middle of the green diamond that is the world is the Glen of Precious Stones. It is in the shape of a heart, and glows like a ruby, though all stones and gems are there. It is there that the Sidhe go to refresh their deathless life."*

Fiona wrote about Columba a good deal and his name crops up frequently in *Carmina Gadelica*. Columba was a historical person, born in Donegal, Ireland, who sailed with a band of followers to Iona in Scotland in 563AD. There he founded a monastery, and for many decades after, his followers travelled Pictland (as Scotland was known then) bringing the new Christian religion to all who would listen. However, the actions of Columba during his long lifetime are not those that usually leap to mind when speaking of an early Christian saint; far from it. He definitely straddled the line between Christian and pre-Christian belief and practice, and was comfortable in so doing. We shall speak of him in other places in this book.

The first point worthy of note in the section quoted above is that this monk, presumably named Oran from the comment at the end of the section, seems to have known where he was going. His determined voyage of heading consistently due North implies that he was making a conscious attempt to reach the Realm of Faery, which, somehow, he knew to be in the frozen North. This is confirmed by the fact that when he eventually arrived there he did not express any surprise, regret or fear, was content to stay, and generally enjoyed himself for three hundred years. If he had been sailing purely on an evangelical mission, then judging by his account of how he spent this three hundred years he clearly soon forgot his raison d'être. Indeed, when he eventually came back to Iona he may not necessarily have totally abandoned his Christian faith but he certainly decided that the Faeries have a thing or two worth incorporating into that religion. This, needless to say, did not go down too well with his ecclesiastical brethren.

The periods he spent sailing – *"thrice seven days … thrice thirty days … thrice three years"* – are symbolic. Whenever we have three, or groups of three, and especially when we have a triple group of threes, we know we are moving from the regular numbering system of the human world and passing into the Realm of Faery. Note the little comment about Iceland being like a small bluebell (or hyacinth) – remember it was among a cluster of hyacinths that William Sharp received his Faery blessing from the Faery Lady of the Sea when he was seven years old.

Next we are told, *"For the first three years the finned things of the sea brought him food; for the second three years he knew the kindness of the creatures of the air; and in the last three years angels fed him."* This emphasises the symbiotic nature of the Realm of Faery where there is no separation or distance between the Faeries, humans and the fauna of this world. This is very important.

As the writer R.J. Stewart has pointed out, there is a three-fold alliance among humans, Faeries and the animal kingdom, and gaining a deeper understanding of this alliance helps a great deal in working successfully with the Faery lore. The finned things of the sea and the creatures of the air crop up again a few times in Fiona's stories concerning Columba, particularly in the story *The Three Marvels of Hy*, to be found in the collection *The Washer of the Ford*, where he is admonished by an angel for not having given his blessing to these creatures. It is not clear if Oran's voyage took place before or after Columba's angelic dressing-down but whichever it was *The Chronicles of the Sidhe* is raising the same point from the Faery point of view. Do not ignore the creatures of water or sea simply because you often cannot see them and cannot easily communicate with them. There is also a deeper symbolic meaning to this in that humans live on the surface of the earth while the creatures of the air tend to be above us and the creatures of the water tend to be below us. We are in-between these two other realms and the state of being in-between was a very magical one to the early Celts.

Next we have the usual motif of Faery time being totally different from what we think we know about time. *"He lived among the Sidhe for three hundred years. When he came back to Iona, he was asked where he had been all that long night since evensong to matins."* There is a factual aspect to this differential in the passing of time, but it also contains a warning of the real danger of the unprepared human visitor to the Realm of Faery becoming ensnared in the glamour of the place, as indeed Oran seems to have been. It is easy to spend too much time there, even in the imagination, to no good purpose. Fiona warned of this several times throughout her thirteen years of writing. For example, in the short story *The Lynn of Dreams* to be found in *The Winged Destiny*, she says,

> *"Dark, pathless glens await the troubled thought of those who cross the dim borderlands. To dwell overlong, there; to listen overlong, there; overlong to speak with those, or to see those whose bright, cold laughter is to us so sad (we know not why), and whose tranquil songs are to us so passing forlorn and wild; overlong to commune with them by the open gate, at the wild wood or near the green mound or by the grey wave; is to sow the moonseed of a fatal melancholy, wherein when it is grown and its poppy-heads stir in a drowsy wind, the mind that wanders there calls upon oblivion as a lost child calling upon God."*

Pay attention to this.

The straightforward wording of the next section almost obscures an important aspect of life in the Realm of Faery. We are told *"He had drunk sweet ale every day, and every day had known love among flowers and green bushes, and at dusk had sung old beautiful forgotten songs, and with star-flame had lit strange fires, and at the full of the moon had gone forth laughing to slay."* This echoes the section from the opening of this tale that says, *"They fight with shadows, and are glad; but the shadows are not shadows to them. The Shee slay great numbers at the full moon ..."*

Note this off-hand, apparently uncaring attitude to slaying. The Sidhe go *"forth laughing to slay ..."* and *"slay great numbers ..."* at the full moon. First, it should be pointed out that this slaying must not be interpreted as killing, in the sense we know it in this world – a final, often violent, act that results in physical death. There is no physical death in the Realm of Faery. But putting aside such arguments for the moment, we must take note of the fact that they do this slaying with pleasure and with no hint of remorse or retribution, or that it is somehow wrong. It is no more than a guiltless and guilt-free past time. So too with the guilt-free daily drinking sessions and love making in the open air. All of these things are enjoyed to the fullest, for their own sake, and with no interference from feelings of guilt or notions of sinning. The Faeries have no knowledge or understanding of abstract human concepts such as guilt or sin. This can explain their sometimes seemingly cruel or uncaring words and actions. Do not expect them to necessarily behave with the same manners or degree of politeness that we expect from our fellow human beings.

Note that later in the tale it is this casual attitude to slaying that the abbot on Iona finds unacceptable and for which, he believes, the Faeries are already in Hell or are at least certainly doomed to be sent there for the rest of eternity. Be aware of this unfettered attitude that the Faeries enjoy and which most of us do not. It can be a hard thing to experience when travelling in the Realm of Faery, or when working on a close magical level with a Faery guide, as it can easily be misunderstood, making them come across as uncaring, emotionally cold and even cruel if you do not keep this in mind.

The comment that Oran then makes as to how the Faeries might be known is interesting. He says, *"away from there they had a cold, cold hand, a cold, still voice, and cold ice-blue eyes."* This tells us specifically that when they leave the Realm of Faery their visual image changes to this rather severe, chilly appearance but, unfortunately, it does not tell us how they look while still in their own realm. This is an important point as it warns you to never take what you see in the Realm of Faery at face value. Things can, and do, change frequently in a manner unknown in this world.

Following his description of the shenanigans he had been getting up to for the past three hundred or so years, Oran then gives a comment on the layout or appearance of the Realm of Faery. He says: *"They had four cities at the four ends of the green diamond that is the world. That in the north was made of earth; that in the east, of air; that in the south, of fire; that in the west, of water."* These four cities are known from early Celtic legend, as quoted above in my comment regarding the Tuatha De Danann. We know their names – Falias, Findias, Murias and Gorias (often found with variant spellings). Fiona commented on them throughout her Faery-oriented writings and, indeed, wrote one poem about all four cities collectively and four other poems about each individual city. See Chapter Nine for a full discussion on these Faery locations.

However there is something new and important in Oran's description of this place. This previously unknown piece of Faery lore is, *"They had four cities at the four ends of the green diamond that is the world … In the middle of the green diamond that is the world is the Glen of Precious Stones. It is in the shape of a heart, and glows like a ruby, though all stones and gems are there. It is there that the Sidhe go to refresh their deathless life."* We have long known of the four cities but the fact they are to be found *"at the four ends of a green diamond that is the world"* is new information and opens up all sorts of possibilities for deeper exploration of these important Faery power sources. The next statement gives even more valuable and previously unknown Faery lore. *"In the middle of the green diamond that is the world is the Glen of Precious Stones. It is in the shape of a heart, and glows like a ruby, though all stones and gems are there."* This short section taken in its entirety, and along with the information we already have about the four cities, gives enough detail and specific imagery to keep the experienced traveller in the Realm of Faery busy for a very long time.

The final statement, *"It is there that the Sidhe go to refresh their deathless life,"* is loaded with all sorts of interpretations and implications. It clearly means that the Glen of Precious Stones is a very important place to all Faeries. It also lets us know that although they live a 'deathless' life it is nonetheless a life that needs some care and maintenance. This leads on to several questions – what happens to Faeries who fail to make a journey to this rejuvenating valley? Do they weaken or fall sick? How often do they need to go there? Exactly how does this place rejuvenate and revitalize the Faeries? Is it enough just to be there, like some ethereal health spa, or does it involve some ritual or ceremony in order to evoke and invoke its rejuvenating powers? Is it a place that we of this world can visit and, if so, what will happen to our vitality and life-energies? Will they too be renewed or, conceivably, would the sheer energy of this place be too much for us to bear? I would argue that Fiona is actively encouraging us to seek this place out. Why else would she have given us so much detail?

The information that the four cities sit at the corners of the green diamond of the Faery world is relevant here, and again raises previously unasked questions. Is their function actually as watchtowers to keep away any non-Faery who may try to access their very important (holy?) Glen of Precious Stones, either to defile it or attempt to use it for their own ends? This is a possibility but it is significant that Fiona makes it clear in her poem *The Dirge of the Four Cities* and the four poems dealing with the four cities individually that they have long been abandoned and are in a state of disrepair. Why? Was this the result of the Tuatha De Danann long ago leaving the far Northern isles of the world, as discussed above? This gives another possible answer to the question of why the Faeries have left their homes in the hollow hills – perhaps they have gone back to the Glen of Precious Stones to rejuvenate.

Incidentally, note the frequent use of precious gems in the poem Gorias (see Chapter Nine). Does this mean that the city of Gorias has more of a direct connection to the Glen of Precious Stones than the other three cities do? Also, if the four cities were watchtowers and are now abandoned, does this mean that access to the Glen of Precious Stones is now open to all? Clearly much serious magical and spiritual work, thought and study is needed to answer these questions. Perhaps this helps you to appreciate how much information Fiona Macleod did actually give to the human world and how difficult it must have been for her to put across such all-encompassing unfamiliar concepts.

The final part of this lengthy quotation from *The Chronicles of the Sidhe* focuses its attention back on Iona amongst the monks of Columba.

> *"The holy monks said that this kingdom was certainly Ifurin, Gaelic Hell. So they put their comrade alive in a grave in the sand, and stamped the sand down upon his head, and sang hymns so that mayhap even yet his soul might be saved, or, at least, that when he went back to that place he might remember other songs than those sung by the milk-white women with eyes like sloes and lips red as rowans.*

'Tell that honey-mouthed cruel people that they are in Hell,' said the abbot, 'and give them my ban and my curse unless they will cease laughing and loving sinfully and slaying with bright lances, and will come out of their secret places and be baptized.'

They have not yet come.

This adventurer of the dreaming mind is another Oran, that fabulous Oran of whom the later Columban legends tell. I think that other Orans go out, even yet, to the Country of the Sidhe. But few come again. It must be hard to find that glen at the heart of the green diamond that is the world; but, when found, harder to return by the way one came."

The treatment meted out by the monks to their fellow holy man is brutal in the extreme. They seem to have rushed to a snap judgment that because the place Oran visited was not of this earth, and because the people there knew how to enjoy themselves without feelings of guilt or sin, it must be the Hell spoken of in the Christian religion. But rather than give Oran a chance to repent and ask forgiveness, which surely would be the 'Christian' thing to do, they grab him and bury him alive in the sand.

This very act, though, mirrors the action taken by the holy St Columba himself on arriving in Iona – but for very different reasons. According to the life of the saint that has come down to us, when he and his followers arrived safely in Iona from Ireland in 563AD they set about building a chapel in which to worship. Before building began Columba declared that a volunteer was needed to be buried alive in the earth over which the new place of Christian worship would be constructed. Hardly what we would call a 'Christian' act! One zealous young monk, called Oran, came forward for the task. He was duly laid in the sand and buried alive. Three days later Columba said that the remains of Oran should be disinterred and given a proper Christian burial. However when they scraped away the sand from the face of the corpse Oran suddenly sat up, alive, and said to Columba, *"Death has no mystery, and Hell is not what you say it is."* The horrified saint immediately decreed that Oran's mouth be stuffed with sand to stop him blabbing further and that the grave be quickly refilled. Visitors to Iona today can still see Reilig Oran (Oran's Cemetery) with its large mound outside the tiny Oran's Chapel. Is the similar account of this act from *The Chronicles of the Sidhe*, albeit with different motivation, the Faeries' version of what really happened to Oran? This may well be an example of both Faeries and humans relating their own versions of a mutual historical incident.

Continuing with Faery version of this gruesome tale we are told the abbot (who is not specifically identified as Columba) said, *"'Tell that honey-mouthed cruel people that they are in Hell … and give them my ban and my curse unless they will cease laughing and loving sinfully and slaying with bright lances, and will come out of their secret places and be baptized.' They have not yet come."* There are two reasons why the Faeries may have ignored the abbot's offer of Christian salvation; either Oran did not return to the Polar Regions because it is not Hell, despite the abbot's assertion, or else Oran did return, gave the Faeries the abbot's offer but they chose to forego Christian baptism and salvation. I think this is the more likely scenario.

Finally we have the statement, mentioned earlier, that few modern-day Orans manage to find the Realm of Faery, and not all of those manage to go on to discover the Glen of Precious Stones. The few who are successful are so changed by the experience that they find it harder to return than it was to discover the glen in the first place. This should not be read as a warning saying "Keep Out!" but rather as a clear statement of fact. If you set out on this spiritual journey there is a very good chance you will fail; are you really ready and able to accept such failure? If you decide you are, you must be prepared for the fact that the experience will be so intense you will never be the same again. This motif is also scattered throughout the Arthurian legends and Celtic and Gaelic folklore.

Hopefully by now you are beginning to understand why Fiona Macleod's Faery writings are so important and how much information can be contained in a few short paragraphs. The Faery book *The Chronicles of the Sidhe* is still available in its entirety in the Realm of Faery. Considering how much useful information was contained in the short section just dealt with, you can begin to see how much Faery lore remains to be disclosed, discovered and made available to interested seekers in our world today. A few shorter examples of the wealth of valuable information concerning the Faeries in general contained within the writings of Fiona Macleod now follow.

In her essay *The Gael and his Heritage* from *The Winged Destiny*, Fiona says:

"When I speak of the Gaelic people of Ireland and Scotland, I speak, alas, only of the small Gaelic remnant in the Scottish Highlands and Isles, and of the remnant in Ireland. This people is unable or unwilling to accept the bitter solace of absorption in the language, the written thought, the active, omnipresent, and

variegated energy of the dominant race. It has to keep silence more and more, and soon it too will be silent. It is a strange thing: that a nation can hold within itself an ancient race, standing for the lost, beautiful, mysterious ancient world, can see it fading through its dim twilight, without heed to preserve that which might yet be preserved, without interest even in that which once gone cannot come again. The old Gaelic race is in its twilight indeed; but now, alas, it is the hastening twilight after the feast of Samhain, when winter is come at last, out of the hills, down the glens, on the four winds of the world."

This short lamentation is referring to the decline in Gaelic culture that was rampant in the late Victorian period. It had started in earnest as early as 1748 when the British government passed The Act of Proscription as a punishment to the Gaelic Highlanders and Islanders who had supported the unsuccessful uprising of Bonnie Prince Charlie in 1745. Part of the provisions of this act of cultural genocide prohibited the wearing of the traditional tartan, the teaching of the written Gaelic language, the playing of the traditional bagpipes, the right to bear arms and the gathering together of the Gaelic people in groups. By the time this terrible Act of Parliament was repealed thirty-eight years later the damage had been done. However it was further exacerbated by the mass clearing of the same Gaelic speakers from their ancient homelands and the enforced migration to the New World, all to make way for sheep.

This total disregard for human life, culture and dignity was bad enough, but Fiona, as a Faery, understood that it greatly affected the Realm of Faery as well. The Gaelic Highlander and Islander have always had a close affinity with the Faeries and whereas the Gaels did not necessarily trust or attempt to befriend the Faeries they did at least acknowledge their existence, their power and, especially, their dignity. As the islands and mainland glens became more and more denuded of the ancient Gaelic people, the Realm of Faery recognised that an ally, albeit an uncomfortable ally, was being lost.

If you substitute the word 'Faery' in the above quotation for the word 'Gaelic' then the sentiments expressed ring just as true and are just as apt. The final sentence, with its reference to Samhain and to the four winds of the world (a purely Faery expression if ever there was one), strongly hints at the real subject of this lamentation being the Faeries just as much as the human Gaels. And all of this emphasises yet again the point strongly made above that the Faeries are disappearing rapidly from our Gaelic and Celtic shores.

Clearly this unhappy subject was one that was on Fiona's mind. She raised it again in a much more specific way in an essay called *The Four Winds of Eirinn*, which can also be found in *The Winged Destiny*. In this piece Fiona says,

> *"The Gentle People have no longer a life common with our own. They have gone beyond grey unvisited hills. They dwell in far islands perhaps, where the rains of Heaven and the foam of the sea guard their fading secrecies. Not here, in any Avalon betwixt the last beaches of the Hebrides and the stones of Carnac, shall that glen be found, that shore be touched, where the old Gaelic world shall live anew. An evil has fallen upon us, that may or may not have been inevitable; that may or may not be from within ourselves as well as from without. It is inevitable now."*

This particular statement of Faery withdrawal is much more bleak and final than her other ones. Note in the second last sentence she raises the question whether this evil may or may not have been inevitable. Does this imply that earlier Faery communicators had tried to warn the human world of what was happening but their cries went unheeded? Whatever she meant, her short, final sentence is clear enough, *"It is inevitable now."* Perhaps I am being unrealistically optimistic when I say I think she is wrong. I believe it is not inevitable and it is indeed reversible. There are still some from the Realm of Faery who are willing to reach out to those of us from the human realm that are capable and willing to listen. Fiona Macleod left enough information concerning the ways, lore, belief and mythology of her native Realm of Faery to keep the sincere and active seeker after Faery truth busy for a long time. I do agree though that this has now become an urgent situation. The decline that she speaks of above has had, and is still having, a devastating effect on the already fragile human-Faery relationships and those of us who care at all for this wonderful and ancient bond must act swiftly to strengthen the few links that remain.

Perhaps this is what she was hinting at in her evocative story *The Anointed Man* from *Under the Dark Star* that deals with the Faeries giving Alasdair Achanna, the hero of the story, the Faery sight. The last short paragraph of this tale talks of the Faery Realm and says, *"But the place is far, and the hour is hidden. No man may seek that for which there can be no quest. Only the wild bees know of it, but I think they must be the bees of Magh-Mell. And there no man that liveth may wayfare — yet."*

That single, final word 'yet' is very interesting and crucial to getting a grasp on the current human-Faery situation. When Fiona wrote this in the 1890s it was at a time when she was painfully aware of the distance that the Faeries had put between them and us, and of how difficult it had become for us to travel to their realm. However the addition of that final word shows that Fiona believed that at some point in the future things would be returned to the way they were. I would argue that 'yet' could be changed to 'until now.' We are at the point in time where access is once again becoming easier. Note that I do not say it is becoming easy, but things are easing up and now is the time to start a serious move in the direction of resuming our ancient alliance with the Realm of Faery.

Note the reference to wild bees. See Chapter Seven for more on these important little creatures.

Finally, in the *Epilogue*, which concludes her collection of short stories *The Dominion of Dreams*, Fiona gives this little snippet of information on how to recognise when you are in the presence of unseen Faeries:

> *"Out of the blue serenities where nothing, not even the moving whiteness of a vanishing wing, was visible; out of the heat and glory of the day; out of that which is beyond — an eddy of wind swiftly descended. I saw the grass shiver along the green path. A few broken sprays and twigs whirled this way and that. In my own land this has one open meaning. Those invisible ones whom we call the hidden people — whom so many instinctively ever reducing what is great to what is small, what is of mystery and tragic wonder to what is fantastic and unthinkable, call 'the fairies' — have passed by. There are too many who inhabit the world that from our eyes is hidden, for us to know who pass, in times, on occasions like this. The children of light and darkness tread the same way."*

The last two sentences sound a note of caution. The stirring of the grass and leaves on a windless day betrays the passing of an unseen people, but it does not betray if they are children of light or children of darkness. If nothing else this reveals once again that there is more than one 'type' of Faery. This is also stated specifically in *The Chronicles of the Sidhe* where we are told that "*Some say it* (the new home of the Sidhe) *is among the pathless mountains of Iceland. But my friend spoke to an Iceland man, and he said he had never seen them. There were Secret People there, but not the Gaelic Sidhe.*" More will be said on the various types of Faery and Secret People as we come across them in Fiona's writings.

Chapter Five

Seumas Macleod

It is the young god who, Seumas the Seer says, was born of human hope, weaned with human tears, taught by dreams and memories, and therewith given for his body Beauty and for his soul, Immortal Joy.

THERE IS AN important character mentioned in several of Fiona's writings based on a real person that William Sharp befriended while still young. This was the Hebridean fisherman Seumas Macleod. The references to him and his teachings are scattered throughout William's letters and Fiona's writings. He is mentioned in Elizabeth Sharp's memoir of her late husband where she says,

> *"In his sixteenth year he [William] was laid low with a severe attack of typhoid fever. It was to that summer during the long months of convalescence in the West that many of his memories of Seumas Macleod belong. Of this old fisherman he wrote, 'When I was sixteen I was on a remote island where he lived, and on the morrow of my visit I came at sunrise upon the old man standing looking seaward with his bonnet removed from his long white locks; and upon my speaking to Seumas (when I saw he was not 'at his prayers') was answered, in Gaelic of course, 'Every morning like this I take my hat off to the beauty of the world.'"*

William said in a letter dated December 30th 1899 to his friend Frank Rinder:

> *"Just a line, dear Frank, both as dear friend and literary comrade, to greet you on New Year's morning, and to wish you health and prosperity in 1900. I would like very much for you to read some of this new Fiona work, especially the opening pages of 'Iona', for they contain a very deep and potent spiritual faith and hope,*

that has been with me ever since, as there told, as a child of seven, old Seumas Macleod (who taught me so much — was indeed the <u>father</u> of Fiona) — took me on his knees one sundown on the island of Eigg, and made me pray to 'Her.' I have never written anything mentally so spiritually autobiographical. Strange as it may seem it is almost all literal reproduction of actuality with only some dates and names altered."

This tells us that William had known Seumas since he was seven years old and that he stayed with him on the Isle of Eigg. This is one of the very few cases where William or Fiona gave a specific location we can identify for Seumas Macleod's home. Usually when Fiona talked of meeting him she used vague phrases like 'on a remote island' or 'while sailing in the Hebrides.' On other occasions she would use names for places that do not exist in our world but may well be actual locations in the Realm of Faery. The curious comment in the letter concerning Seumas being Fiona's father is dealt with in detail in my biography of William Sharp, *The Little Book of the Great Enchantment*.

Seumas features in Fiona's first published work, *Pharais: A Romance of the Isles*, which deals with a tragic love affair between Lora and Alastair. Much of this story is based on William's early life, the 'Alastair' of the tale being William. One passage describes how Alastair learned much from Seumas. Note the similarity between the factual account quoted in the first paragraph above and the fictional account that follows.

"It was from Seumas that Alastair [William], in boyhood and youth, had learned much, not only of his store of legends and ancient runes and Old Celtic poetry, but also of that living poetry which makes the heart of the Gael more tender than that of other men, and his brain more wrought with vision. From him he had first heard how that for one to have died is to have 'gone into the silence'; that for an old man or woman to pass away in extreme age is to 'have the white sleep'; that for a fisherman to drown is for him to have 'the peace of the quiet wave.' Seumas had filled his brain with lovely words — lovely in themselves and in their meaning; but he had made his clansman a poet by one thing he did and said. For once ... he went to Ithona to stay for some weeks. At sunrise on the morrow of his arrival, on his coming out upon the grass which sloped to the shore a few yards away, he saw Seumas standing, with his wide, blue bonnet in his hand, and the sun shining full upon his mass of white hair — not praying, as at first Alastair thought, but with a rapt look on his face, and with glad, still-youthful eyes gazing lovingly upon the sea. 'What is it, Seumas?' he had asked; and the old isleman, turning to him

with a grave smile, had answered, 'Morning after morning, fair weather or foul, after I have risen from my prayers and ere I have broken fast, I come here and remove my hat and bow my head, with joy and thanksgiving, before the Beauty of the world.' From that day, the world became a new world for Alastair."

The first two references to Seumas in *Pharais* are rather oblique. Lora, the heroine of the tale, is gazing towards the sea for a glimpse of the steamer bringing her husband back to her. The tale relates that she *"saw there the soul of the Ocean gloriously arisen. Beneath the weedy slabs of rock whereon she stood, the green of the sea-moss lent a yellow gleam to the slow-waving dead-man's-hair which the tide laved to and fro sleepily, as though the bewitched cattle of Seumas the Seer were drowsing there unseen, known only of their waving tales, swinging silently as the bulls dreamed of the hill-pastures they should see no more."*

Here Fiona is referring to a story concerning Seumas 'the Seer' as she called him, who has enchanted a herd of cattle to live with him beneath the waves. She says no more of this tale. It is not a story from Celtic mythology and is our first hint that Seumas is a Faery as the realm of Faery is often referred to as Tir-fo-Tuinn, meaning the land under the waves. Later Fiona refers to the Seumas again when Mary, another female character in the novel, spots Lora's husband Alastair and thinks to herself, *"It is the young god ... who, Seumas the Seer says, was born of human hope, weaned with human tears, taught by dreams and memories, and therewith given for his body Beauty ... and for his soul, Immortal Joy."* Note that this god was made from human 'parts' – hope and tears – whereas in other world mythologies it is the gods who made us. We are not given the name of 'the young god' but whoever he is, this is not a description to be found in Celtic mythology. He is from the Realm of Faery.

Towards the end of this book Fiona wrote a longer piece that in part says of Seumas:

"The old isleman had never once been on the mainland; though in his youth he had sailed along its endless coasts. Tall and strong he was, despite his great age; and his eyes were the eyes of a young man who hears his first-born laughing and crooning against its mother's breast. Ignorant as he was of the foreign tongue of the mainland, ignorant of books and unable to read even a verse in the Gaelic Scriptures of which he knew so many chapters by heart, he was yet strong in knowledge and wise in the way of it beyond most men. For he knew all that is to be known concerning the island and the surrounding sea, and what moved thereon and lived therein; and, in his humbleness and simplicity, he saw so deep into the

human heart and into the mystery of the soul, that he was not ashamed to know he was man, nor to pray to God to guide him through the shadows."

Fiona names several locations in *Pharais* that we can positively identify in Scotland but she also gives names to some islands unknown in this world. One such place is called Ithona and is said to be the home of Seumas Macleod. If this were a Gaelic word it would be pronounced in a manner very similar to Iona and, as commented earlier, the Isle of Iona is a Faery gateway. Of Ithona she says, *"Upon Ithona no one dwelt other than an old islander whose fathers had been there before him for generations. Seumas Macleod was at once shepherd and fisherman, and caretaker of the long, low farm-house."*

Another island named in the story but unknown in this world is I-na-Trilleachan-trahad, which translates as 'the Island of the Oyster-Catcher at Ebb Tide.' The oyster-catcher is a bird sacred to Brigid, and in Gaelic this shore-bird is known as the 'servant of Brigid'. Brigid is one of the few goddesses that appear in Celtic mythology, Faery mythology and Christian sainthood. The reference to ebb tide brings up the notion of the important 'in-between' places, as mentioned earlier in this book, which are recognised gateways to the Realm of Faery.

These islands are Faery locations. Understanding this, and understanding what their names mean, shows clearly that Seumas Macleod was not of this world. It also demonstrates how easily Fiona got the people, places and events of her native Faery world mixed up with those of our physical world. Perhaps this was deliberate, perhaps not, but it warns us to read everything she wrote very carefully and to read it twice – from the Faery point of view and from the human point of view. Both readings will reveal much.

So important was Seumas Macleod to the man William Sharp and to the Faery Fiona Macleod that Fiona dedicated an entire essay to this Faery fisherman, entitled simply *Seumas: A Memory*. It can be found in the volume of her collected works called *The Winged Destiny: Studies in the Spiritual History of the Gael*. I give it here in full as it contains important Faery lore and is a typical example of how Fiona passed on this first-hand Faery information in the guise of a vignette from her life.

"I have again and again, since my first book 'Pharais', alluded to Seumas Macleod: and as I have shown in the sketch called 'Barabal' and in the dedication

to the volume entitled 'The Divine Adventure' it is to this old Highlander, as well as to my Hebridean nurse Barabal, that I owe more than to any other early influences.

Let me tell one other story of him, which I have meant often to tell, but have as often forgotten.

He had gone once to the Long Island [the Isles of Lewis and Harris in the Outer Hebrides], with three fishermen, in their herring-coble. The fish had been sold and the boat had sailed southward to a Lews haven where Seumas had a relative. The younger men had 'hanselled' their good bargain over well, and were laughing and talking freely as they walked up the white road from the haven. Something was said that displeased Seumas greatly, and he might have spoken swiftly in reproof; but just then a little naked child ran laughing from a cottage, chased by his smiling mother. Seumas caught up the child, who was but an infant, and set him in their midst, and then kneeled and said the few words of a Hebridean hymn beginning; "even as a little child, most holy, pure..." No more was said, but the young men understood; and he who long after told me of this episode added that though he had often since acted weakly and spoken foolishly, he had never, since that day, uttered foul words. Another like characteristic anecdote of Seumas (as the skipper who made his men cease mocking a 'fool') I have told in the tale called 'The Amadan' in 'The Dominion of Dreams.'

I remember asking him once — as simply as one might ask about the tides, or the weather — what he thought of the elements. And he answered as simply. 'Fire is God's touch,' he said: 'and light is God Himself: and water is the mother of life.' I asked him if he thought all the old gods were dead. He asked why. I said that he had just spoken of water as the mother of life, and yet that he had often told me of legends of Mânan, the god of the sea.

'No,' he answered, 'they are not all dead. They think <u>we</u> are. They do not change. They are very patient, the old ancient gods. Perhaps it is because they do not care at all, no, not a whistle of the wind, for what we think or what we do.'

'But,' he added, 'some have died. And some are very old, and are sleeping, till they get their youth again.'

'And Mânan ... does <u>he</u> live?'

'Ay, for sure. He was here before Christ came. He will see the end of all endings. They say he sleeps in the hollows of great oceans, and sits on mountain-bergs of ice at the Pole, chanting an old ancient chant.'

Another time I asked him why he had never married. 'There is only one love,' he said simply, 'and that I gave to the woman of my love. But she died of a fever when I was down with it too. That was in Skye. When I got up, my heart was in her grave. I would be very young, then: but I had too much life put away. And *then,' he added, with a smile half whimsical, half wistful, 'to marry a woman for comfort or for peace is only for those who haven't the way of the one or the power to make the other.' I am glad to know that another is hardly less indebted to old Seumas Macleod. I am not permitted to mention his name, but a friend and kinsman allows me to tell this: that when he was about sixteen he was on the remote island where Seumas lived, and on the morrow of his visit came at sunrise upon the old man, standing looking seaward with his bonnet removed from his long white locks; and upon his speaking to Seumas (when he saw that he was not 'at his prayers') was answered, in Gaelic of course, 'every morning like this I take off my hat to the beauty of the world.'*

The untaught islander who could say this had learned an ancient wisdom, of more account than wise books, than many philosophies.

I could write much of this revered friend — so shrewd and genial and worldly-wise, for all his lonely life; so blithe in spirit and swiftly humorous; himself a poet, and remembering countless songs and tales of old; strong and daring, on occasion; good with the pipes, as with the nets; seldom angered, but then with a fierce anger, barbaric in its vehemence; a loyal clansman; in all things, good and not so good, a Gael of the Isles."

The middle section of this short memoir is important. It is brief but tells us a good deal about the Faery gods and, importantly, how they view us. Fiona starts this section with an interesting statement: *"I remember asking him once — as simply as one might ask about the tides, or the weather — what he thought of the elements."* This seems like a very odd question to ask the skipper of a small herring boat. Asking of the tides or weather, yes, both relevant and both concerning things that you would expect a fisherman to have knowledge of, but to ask his thoughts on the elements would be considered out of the normal. However Seumas accepts the question without comment or puzzle and gives his answer. *"'Fire is God's touch,' he said: 'and light is God Himself: and water is the mother of life.'"* It turns out the answer is even more confusing than the question but Fiona accepts it without comment or the need for further clarification.

It is confusing because Seumas only mentions three elements, whereas in our world we accept that there are four. Threes and fours are important throughout the Faery and human traditions and will be discussed throughout the text of this book. But note what the three elements are – fire, light and water. Only two of these, fire and water, are amongst our familiar four elements, the other two being earth and air. Clearly Seumas's understanding of the elements is not based on anything physical at all, but this should be expected, as he, being a Faery, was not from this physical world.

Two of the Faery elements, fire and light, are directly connected with God (for which read all Faery gods and goddesses) and are component parts of each other. The third, water, is stated to be the mother of life, presumably Faery life as well as physical life. This may explain why so many of Fiona's stories deal with water in one way or another. Many, like this one, are set in boats, fishing villages or cottages near the sea while many feature lochs, rivers, pools and waterfalls. Others deal with drowning, swimming, the movement of the waves and tides, seals and fishes, and 'The Land Under Waves' of Faery. There is a whole realm of Faery magic concerning the Faeries of water that has hardly been looked at. We tend to concentrate on the Faeries of the Green World because the Green World is also our own human habitat and source of food and shelter. We do not live in the sea. We can travel rather clumsily over it, but we do not move through it in the way we daily move through the Green World. Fiona spent a lot of effort trying to point out to the seeker after the Realm of Faery to look to the waters as well as the forests, mountains and valleys of the dry land we walk daily.

There is an interesting passage in *Carmina Gadelica* dealing with what was known as Frìth: that is, loosely, divination or augury. Carmichael recorded a common belief amongst the Gaelic islanders that,

> *"To make the frìth across stream, lake, or sea is difficult, and across a wide or deep sea most difficult. The Siol Sidh (Race of Faeries) has more power under water than above water, under the foundations of the sea than under the foundations of the land; and the Siol Sidh interferes with the current of man's thoughts and thwarts man's mind and wishes. The sea is more sacred and mysterious than the land, and contains inhibiting spirits not known ashore; therefore, an informant said, the frìth cannot so well be made across the sea 'because there is a sort of fairies under the sea, and the frìth is hard to read.'"*

There is much work yet to be done with regard to the Faeries of water. Fiona spent a great deal of time and effort pointing out their importance to us. This excerpt also shows that in the Victorian era the islanders of the Outer Hebrides still knew of this important connection between Faeries and the sea, yet we in our modern age have all but forgotten it. How much more important Faery lore has slipped from the common memory over the past century or so?

Fiona's next question to Seumas is one that anyone interested in learning more of the Faeries would love to ask. *"I asked him if he thought all the old gods were dead."* This time his answer is much more straightforward and revealing. *"'No,' he answered, 'they are not all dead. They think <u>we</u> are. They do not change. They are very patient, the old ancient gods. Perhaps it is because they do not care at all, no, not a whistle of the wind, for what we think or what we do.'"*

This is important and needs to be expanded upon for its full significance and ramifications to sink in. He makes it very clear that the Faery gods are, for the most part, still alive but, for some reason, they think that humankind is dead. Why? Do they mean dead in the physical sense or do they mean dead in the sense that we are unaware of the Realm of Faery, that we are 'dead' to that connection between the worlds that our ancestors used to enjoy?

Considering the number of stories, from both human and Faery mythology, concerning contact between the two I am sure the Faeries know perfectly well that humankind is still alive. But considering that the vast majority of humankind has no knowledge or awareness of the Realm of Faery, and how this important and powerful place and race has been so trivialized in the modern mind and imagery, it is easy to see how the Faeries would consider us totally dead to their world intellectually and emotionally. This is a tragic situation for both Faery and human. The Faery Fiona Macleod was aware of this and made strident efforts to reveal the Realm of Faery, all aspects of it, to humankind in the hope of reestablishing that which has been lost. It is for that same reason that this present work is being presented to you now.

Seumas's comment, *"they do not care at all, no, not a whistle of the wind, for what we think or what we do"* may come as a surprise to those who are already familiar with Faeries and the Realm of Faery but it is a hard fact and a very important one to keep in mind when working magically and intuitively with Faeries. This uncaring attitude is mentioned again in Fiona's essay *Iona* where she relates a story of a human woman who fell in love with a Faery man. The woman became pregnant and when her time was near it was clear she was dying. Her Faery lover came to her and said the following to his dying bride, *"'I can't give you life,' he said, 'unless you'll come away with me.' But she would not; for she wished the child to have a Christian baptism. 'Well, goodbye,' he said, 'but you are a weak love. A woman should care more for her lover than for her child.'"* Hardly a happy ending to what had been up until then a beautiful love affair!

Unfortunately the 'Disney' image of the Faery godmother benevolently bestowing three wishes at the wave of a tinsel-covered wand has become so synonymous with fairies that many sincere seekers after the true Faeries come with this unconscious assumption of finding a gentle, caring and all-considerate race of beings. They *can* be convinced to drop their hard attitude and they can become extremely loyal and supportive allies, but the student of Faery must understand that this is always a long, slow and difficult process. It is exactly what happens in our own human world when anthropologists make contact with a previously unknown indigenous people. The indigenous people are at first wary, often scared and unsure of these strangers but through a long, slow and arduous process a mutual acceptance can be achieved which can lead on to full cooperation in time. Seumas's short, sharp answer may stop us in our tracks but it had to be said.

His next comment is also a surprise. *"'But,' he added, 'some have died. And some are very old, and are sleeping, till they get their youth again.'"* Some have died? Does this mean that Faeries are mortal? If so why does he go on to say that others are sleeping "till they get their youth again" – presumably in the Glen of Precious Stones discussed earlier? There are clearly deep mysteries here.

I commented above on the importance of the element of water to the Realm of Faery. Fiona's final question and Seumas's final answer in this short interchange emphasizes this again. Fiona asked, *"'And Mânan … does he live?'"* and Seumas's answer was, *"'Ay, for sure. He was here before Christ came. He will see the end of all endings. They say he sleeps in the hollows of great oceans, and sits on mountain-bergs of ice at the Pole, chanting an old ancient chant.'"*

Students of Celtic mythology will recognise Mânan as being the Celtic god of the sea called Manannan. This early god is sometimes mixed in with the pantheon of Celtic gods and goddesses known collectively as the Tuatha De Danann, but there has long been a teaching that Manannan is of the Faeries and should not be considered one of the Tuatha De Danann, the original race of gods and goddesses that came to the physical world long ago. This is borne out by the Celtic legend that says when the Tuatha De Danann accepted it was time for them to withdraw from the world of humankind they asked Manannan to allot a hollow hill to each of them where they could dwell unseen and unimpeded by the human race. The reason they asked Manannan to do this was because he was not one of their kin and would therefore be an impartial distributor of the best and worst dwelling places. Manannan did not need to reserve a hollow hill for himself as his domain had always been the sea, where according to Seumas, he still lives.

Note the reference to icebergs and the Pole. Once again a Faery is pointing out the importance of the Arctic and the remotest northern islands of this world. Just as there remains much Faery research to be done in connection with water, so too is there much Faery research to be done on the Arctic, icebergs and the North Pole region.

The essay finishes with yet another telling of the early morning meeting when William Sharp saw Seumas Macleod take off his bonnet as a sign of respect for the beauty of the day. This simple vignette points out the importance of taking a moment each day to stop all activity, thought and action and just spend a while in appreciation of the beauty, mystery and wonder of our world and of the Realm of Faery. The regular practice of such simple little rituals adds considerably to our ability to work closely with the Faeries.

In her essay *Iona* Fiona relates a little bit more of the nature of Seumas Macleod. At the point she introduces Seumas she has been discussing with a young priest the old Gaelic belief that the Redeemer will be born as a woman on the Inner Hebridean Isle of Iona. She then says:

> "The other who spoke to me of this Woman who is to save was an old fisherman of a remote island of the Hebrides, and one to whom I owe more than to any other spiritual influence in my childhood, for it was he who opened to me the three gates of Beauty. Once this old man, Seumas Macleod, took me with him to a lonely haven in the rocks, and held me on his knee as we sat watching the sun sink and the moon climb out of the eastern wave. I saw no one, but abruptly he rose and put me from him, and bowed his grey head as he bowed before one who suddenly was standing in that place. I asked eagerly who it was. He told me that it was an Angel. Later, I learned (I remember my disappointment that the beautiful vision was not winged with great white wings) that the Angel was one soft flame of pure white, and that below the soles of his feet were curling scarlet flames. He had come in answer to the old man's prayer. He had come to say that we could not see the Divine One whom we awaited. 'But you will see that Holy Beauty,' said the Angel, and Seumas believed, and I too believed, and believe. He took my hand, and I knelt beside him, and he bade me repeat the words he said. And that was how I first prayed to Her who shall yet be the Balm of the World."

These brief excerpts from just a few of Fiona's writings contain a wealth of Faery mythology that will take a good deal of thought, meditation and magical working to fully realise and understand. For the moment though, the important point to note is that Seumas Macleod has given this knowledge to us. He is an important Faery contact and is one of the few who is keen to work closely with humankind in the revelation of the Faery Mysteries. He, unlike most of his fellow Faeries, does not consider humankind to be dead.

One final personal comment on Seumas Macleod: on January 21st 2009 Seumas Macleod told me that originally he was going to be the person that would write through William Sharp, but as William Sharp grew older and matured from boyhood to adulthood it became clear that a female Faery would be more compatible with his sensitive nature and fragile health, so Seumas stood aside in favour of Fiona. This also strengthens in a symbolic way the fact that Seumas was Fiona's father. He added that he still wants to tell the human world what he can of Faery and wants a 'host' through which to write.

Chapter Six

Faery Gods and Goddesses

In the mythology of the Gael are three forgotten deities, children of Delbaith-Dana. These are Seithoir, Teithoir and Keithoir. One dwells throughout the sea, and beneath the soles of the feet of another are the highest clouds; and these two may be held sacred for the beauty they weave for the joy of eye and ear. But now that, as surely none may gainsay, Keithoir is blind and weary, let us worship at his fane rather than give all our homage to the others.

T HROUGHOUT HER WRITINGS Fiona makes scattered references to the gods and goddesses of the Faeries. By that I mean the gods and goddesses *the Faeries believe in* and hold sacred, as opposed to any of *our* gods or goddesses that we may deem to be from the Realm of Faery. There is not a great deal we can say about them from these little bits and pieces but she has given us enough for us to say with certainty it is a pantheon previously unknown to us. None of the names of these gods and goddesses are familiar to us, none of their legends and myths are to be found in the world mythology of humankind, but, in her usual frustrating manner, Fiona writes of them without detail or explanation as if we are already as conversant with them as she is. But at least she has given out enough names and enough scraps of mythology that we can start to piece together a rather fragmentary base upon which to start some research. Nowhere, though, does she make any reference to exactly how the Faeries regard their deities. Do they hold them in awe, do they perform acts of worship out of respect or fear of these gods and goddesses, do they dwell apart in some special place or are they rubbing shoulders on a daily basis with the Faeries in the Realm of Faery? We are left to do our own research and draw our own conclusions on this subject.

In Chapter Seven we shall take a look at the more important passages Fiona gave us concerning the myths and legends of the Faeries themselves, but in this chapter I shall give what little information we have concerning the individual gods and goddesses that she specifically names and where in her writings you can find these references. One point to consider is the fact that Fiona did not make a 'big deal' out of the Faery gods and goddesses. The way that they are referred to in a very off-hand manner implies that they are not generally considered by the Faeries as figures that inspire great awe, love or even fear. They exist, they become involved from time to time in the daily affairs of the Faeries, they cause some upset for the Faeries from time to time, and that is it. It all seems quite normal, mundane, run-of-the-mill.

If Fiona's attitude towards them is typical of most Faeries then it seems fair to assume that there is no religion-based, institutionalised and formal recognition of the gods and goddesses as superior beings, as is the case with most of humankind's attitude towards our many gods and goddesses. Most of the formal religions of this world create a gap, a separation, between Godhead and humans – they are up there, we are down here. This does not seem to be the case with Faery gods and goddesses who, according to Fiona's accounts, mingle freely with the Faeries in general.

The Awakening of Angus Òg in *The Winged Destiny*, which also appears under the title *The Snow-Sleep of Angus Ogue* in the *Evergreen: Book of Winter*, is an important story in that it introduces Orchil, the Faery weaver goddess who sits at her loom in a subterranean chamber. The events described in this myth reveal her importance to both Faery and human. This short story is a good example of a Faery myth that easily and seamlessly mixes Faery gods with Celtic gods. As well as introducing the Faery goddess Orchil the story also involves the Faery god Keithoir in the company of the Gaelic Celtic god Manannan and the rather obscure Breton Celtic god Hesus. The easy flow of conversation and events amongst these gods and goddess works so well that it raises the question, are they in fact all from the same source, from the same mythology, and if so, is that the mythology of the Faeries? Were the early Celts so close to the Realm of Faery that they treated some Faery deities as their own and, through time, we have forgotten their true origin?

When the story opens the attention is on the Gaelic Celtic god Angus Ogue, who is sleeping on an open, sun-baked hillside in the

Highlands of Scotland. After a lengthy description of where Angus lies, and that he thinks he is alone and unseen, we learn:

"Yet there were eyes to see, for Orchil lifted up her gaze from where she dreamed her triple dream beneath the heather. The goddess ceased from her weaving at the loom of life and death, and looked long at Angus Ogue — Angus, the fair god, the ever young, the lord of love, of music, of song.

'Is it time that he slept indeed?' she murmured, after a long while, wherein she felt the hot blood redden her pale lips and the pulse in her quiet veins leap like a caged bird.

But while she still pondered this thing, three old druids came over the shadow of the hill, and advanced slowly to where the Yellow-haired One lay adream. These, however, she knew to be no mortals, but three of the ancient gods.

When they came upon Angus Ogue they sought to wake him, but Orchil had breathed a breath across a granite rock and blown the deep, immemorial age of it upon him, so that even the speech of the elder gods was no more in his ears than a gnat's idle rumour.

'Awake,' said Keithoir, and his voice was as the tempestuous sigh of pine-forests when winds surge from the pole.

'Awake,' said Manannan, and his voice was as the hollow booming of the sea.

'Awake,' said Hesus, and his voice was as the rush of the green world through space, or as the leaping of the sun …

But Angus stirred not …

'He will awake no more,' murmured Keithoir …

'He will awake no more,' murmured Manannan …

'He will awake no more,' murmured Hesus …

Orchil smiled. 'They are old, old, the ancient gods,' she whispered. 'They are so old they cannot see eternity at rest. For Angus Ogue is the god of Youth, and he only is eternal and unchanging.' Then, before she turned once more to her loom of life and death, she lifted her eyes till her gaze pierced the brown earth and rose above the green world and was a trouble amid the quietudes of the sky. Thereat the icy stars gave forth snow, and Angus Ogue was wrapped in a white shroud that was not as that which melts in the flame of noon …

A thousand years passed, and when for the thousandth time the wet green smell of the larches drifted out of Winter into Spring, Orchil lifted her eyes from where she spun at her loom of life and death. For, over the shoulder of the hill came three old druids, advancing slowly to where the Yellow-haired One lay adream beneath the snow.

'Awake, Angus!' cried Keithoir.

'Awake, Angus!' cried Manannan.

'Awake, Angus!' cried Hesus.

'Awake, awake!' they cried, 'for the world has suddenly grown chill and old.'

Then Orchil put down the shuttle of mystery wherewith she wove the threads of her loom and spoke, 'O ye ancient gods, answer me this. Keithoir, if death were to come to thee, what would happen?'

'The green world would wither as a dry leaf, and as a dead leaf be blown idly before the wind that knows not whither it bloweth.'

'Manannan, if death were to come to thee, what would happen?'

'The deep seas would dry up, O Orchil: there would be sand falling in the place of the dews, and at last the world would reel and fall into the abyss.'

'Hesus, if death were to come to thee, what would happen?'

'There would be no pulse at the heart of the earth, O Orchil, no lift of any star against any sun. There would be a darkness and a silence.'

Then Orchil laughed. 'And yet,' she said, 'when Angus Ogue had the snow-sleep of a thousand years, none knew it! For a thousand years the pulse of his heart of love has been the rhythmic beat of the world … the breath of his nostrils has been as the coming of Spring in the human heart … the breath of his life has been warm against the lips of lovers … the memory of these have been sweet against oblivion.'

'Who is he?' cried Keithoir, 'Is he older than I, who saw the green earth born?'

'Who is he?' cried Manannan, 'Is he older than I, who saw the first waters come forth out of the void?'

'Who is he?' cried Hesus, 'Is he older than I, who saw the first comet wander from the starry fold; who saw the moon when it was a flaming sun, and the sun when it was a seven-fold intolerable flame?'

'He is older!' said Orchil. 'He is the soul of the gods.'

And with that she blew a frith across the palm of her hand, and took away the deep immemorial age of the granite that was upon the Fair God.

'Awake, eternal Spring!' she cried. And Angus awoke, and laughed with joy; and at his laughing the whole green earth was veiled in a snow of blossom.

'Arise, eternal Youth!' she cried. And Angus arose and smiled; and at his smiling the old brown world was clad in dewy green, and everywhere the beauty of the world was sweet against the eyes of young and old, and everywhere the pulse of love leaped in beating hearts.

'Go forth eternal Hope!' she cried. And Angus Ogue passed away on the sun flood, weaving rainbows as he went, that were fair upon the hills of age and light within the valleys of sorrow, and were everywhere a wild, glad joy."

Take note of the use of the words 'sorrow' and 'joy' in the final sentence. We shall take a closer look at these in Chapter Ten.

The first confirmation we get that Orchil is an important and powerful goddess is when she asks herself, *'Is it time that he* (Angus) *slept indeed?'* This implies that she controls the passing of events and, indeed, the actions of the gods themselves. It is as if she had been so focused on her weaving that she did not even notice that Angus had fallen asleep without her bidding. The rest of the tale expands on this theme by the way she clearly knows more than the other gods in the tale and she can control how they behave.

Once again there is a subtle reference to the Arctic and far North when Keithoir first speaks and his voice is described as being like a surge of wind, *'from the pole.'* This theme of the importance of the Northern Polar Region occurs throughout her thirteen years of writing. There is much research still needing to be done on this subject. Also, the common theme of time passing differently in the Realm of Faery than in our world is repeated when the three old druids try to awaken Angus for the second time and they say, *"... the world has suddenly grown chill and old"* when in fact 'suddenly' refers to a period of one thousand years here on earth.

A little further on Orchil echoes the comment made in Chapter Five by Seumas Macleod about the gods needing rest and rejuvenation, when she says, *"They are old, old, the ancient gods... They are so old they cannot see eternity at rest. For Angus Ogue is the god of Youth, and he only is eternal and unchanging."* This also makes it clear that Angus is somehow of a different order of deity for only he is unaffected by the passing of the great aeons and only he maintains his strength without the need of rejuvenation. He is also one of the few gods to be found in both the Faery tradition and the Celtic tradition. It is interesting though that at first it seems this is a story of Angus, yet on further reading it becomes clear that he basically does very little but causes the other, older gods to question who they are and what their purposes are. His importance is stressed again by Orchil towards the end of the tale when she says of him, *"He is the soul of the gods."* Quite an accolade!

The god Hesus is a rather obscure deity known from early Gallic, or Breton, Celtic sources. There are some contemporary comments on him from Roman writers, plus there are some known archaeological artifacts bearing his name and image. Most of these sources portray him as a woodcutter and perhaps a god of the animals and forest but note that here Hesus is connected with the stars and cosmos. This strongly implies that his origins are from Faery and not from Celtic mythology. There are no Celtic gods or goddesses who are connected to the stars, comets or the cosmos. They are all fairly and squarely earth-based. A god or goddess who is cosmically aware does not fit in with Celtic mythology, nor with the mind-set of the early Celts who expressed no interest in anything other than what was happening on earth. The fact that the mythology of the Faeries has an ancient god who was around at the birth of the stars and planets shows that the Faeries were well aware of cosmic things long before the modern Celts were. On a different note, it is worth pointing out that William Sharp's lover, Edith Wingate Rinder was a writer and translator of, amongst other things, old Breton tales and folklore. She would most likely have been familiar with the name Hesus. After meeting Edith, William also became interested in the Breton people and their culture.

Manannan, however, *is* a prominent figure in Celtic mythology, and as is made clear here, is the god of the sea as discussed previously in Chapter Five. There are hints though that his origin may also be from Faery. He appears mainly, although not exclusively, in the group of Celtic tales known collectively as the Mythological Cycle. This, as the name suggests, is the main corpus of Gaelic Celtic myths and legends surrounding the old gods and goddesses. But within that framework Manannan does not quite seem to fit in. He is not specifically named as having come from 'the Northern Islands of the World' as many of the other gods and goddesses were, and when it came time for those other deities to be allocated their own, individual earth mound dwellings they chose Manannan to make the allocation because he was not one of them and would be an impartial mediator.

Fiona says even more on this subject and introduces yet more previously unknown Faery lore in a passage from her essay *Iona* that at first appears to be dealing with the Christian St. Michael.

> "St. Michael is on the surface a saint of extraordinary powers and the patron of the shores and the shore-folk: deeper, he is an angel, who is upon the sea what the angelic saint, St. George, is upon the land: deeper, he is a blending of the Roman Neptune and the Greek Poseidon: deeper, he is himself an ancient Celtic god: deeper, he is no other than Manannan, the god of ocean and all waters, in the Gaelic pantheon: as, once more, Manannan himself is dimly revealed to us as still more ancient, more primitive, and even as supreme in remote godhead, the Father of an Immortal Clan."

Note the repeated use of the word 'deeper', which, as commented on elsewhere in this book, means 'Faery.' The term 'Immortal Clan' is from the Gaelic and means the Faeries.

This is an extraordinary passage and clearly emphasises the importance of St. Michael in the Faery, Celtic and Christian traditions. He is often connected with high places in the Christian tradition, and three prominent centres in Europe that are dedicated to him – Mont St. Michel in France, St. Michael's Mount in Cornwall, and Skellig Michael in Ireland – are all indeed high places. But they are also connected with the sea. Mont St. Michel is twice a day inundated by the incoming tides on the borders between Normandy and Brittany – a Celtic region; St. Michael's Mount sits on a narrow peninsula that juts out into the English Channel from Cornwall – another Celtic region; and Skellig Michael consists of two high, rocky outcrops that rise sheer from the waters of the Atlantic off the south-west coast of Ireland – yet another Celtic country. Anyone interested in learning the Faery tradition to its fullest would do well to study the lives of the early Celtic saints and the places they are connected with.

The third old Druid named in the above tale is Keithoir, who is without doubt solely from the Faery tradition, his name being previously unknown in the mythologies of this world. From what the narrative tells us it is clear he is a god of the Green World, of the earth, the plants and animals. This is borne out by other references to him that Fiona made throughout her writings. Indeed he is mentioned in the dedication to Edith Wingate Rinder in Fiona's first book *Pharais*.

Edith Wingate Rinder was very much the catalyst that William Sharp needed to allow Fiona Macleod to 'come through' and reveal her Faery teachings, hence the dedication to her in Fiona's first book. Part of that dedication contains the following intriguing passage:

"In the mythology of the Gael are three forgotten deities, children of Delbaith-Dana. These are Seithoir, Teithoir and Keithoir. One dwells throughout the sea, and beneath the soles of the feet of another are the highest clouds; and these two may be held sacred for the beauty they weave for the joy of eye and ear. But now that, as surely none may gainsay, Keithoir is blind and weary, let us worship at his fane rather than give all our homage to the others. For Keithoir is the god of the earth: dark-eyed, shadowy brother of Pan; and his fane is among the lonely glens and mountains and lonelier isles of 'Alba cona lingataibh.' It is because you and I are of the children of Keithoir that I wished to grace my book with your name."

Two other gods with very similar names, Seithoir and Teithoir, are mentioned in connection with Keithoir, and this implies that he is part of a trinity of gods. This is not uncommon in the Celtic tradition. But Fiona immediately dismisses Seithoir and Teithoir as being unimportant and barely makes reference to them again in the rest of her writings.

A short comment of a linguistic nature is appropriate here: it has been argued by some that this trinity of gods could be an old, forgotten group from the early Gaelic tradition rather than a previously unknown Faery group. But there is no letter 'K' in the Gaelic alphabet, and William Sharp and Fiona Macleod were both Gaelic speakers. Had Fiona been referring to an early Gaelic god she would almost certainly have changed the spelling to 'Ceithoir' but by deliberately keeping this non-Gaelic spelling she is highlighting the fact that Keithoir is solidly from the Faery tradition, not the Celtic. This reference to Keithoir specifically states he is a god of the earth, as we surmised from the tale related above. However here Fiona states he is blind and weary as if he is getting too old and tired to carry on with his godly tasks. This is an interesting concept and one that she repeated in various ways and in other places.

Note that the last sentence, *"It is because you and I are of the children of Keithoir that I wished to grace my book with your name"* implies that Edith Wingate Rinder was as much of the Faery as Fiona is. If this were the case then it would explain why Edith Wingate Rinder had such a powerful emotional and spiritual effect on William Sharp and why she was such a catalyst for Fiona. This apparent recognition of a fellow Faery, or at least a human with Faery blood, was repeated again in another dedication to another female friend. The *Prologue* to Fiona's book *The Washer of the Ford* is dedicated to 'Kathia' who was Catherine Janvier, a long-time friend and confidant of William Sharp. Part of this lengthy prologue says,

> *"The same blood is in our veins, a deep current somewhere beneath the tide that sustains us. We have meeting places that none knows of; we understand what few can understand; and we share in common a strange and inexplicable heritage. It is you, who are called Kathia of the Sunway, are also Kathia nan Ciar, Kathia of the Shadow, it is because you are what you are that I inscribe this book to you. In it you will find much that is familiar to you … I would like it to be associated with you, to whom not only the mystery but the pagan sentiment and the old barbaric emotion are so near."*

The sentiments expressed here of there being a blood-bond between Fiona Macleod and Catherine Janvier are the same as those expressed above to Edith Wingate Rinder. There is a good deal of esoteric research and work being done on this whole subject of mixed blood-lines and we shall meet this theme again throughout this present book.

But to return to Keithoir: the story *Cathal of the Woods* from *The Washer of the Ford* has a section where the green spirits of the trees ask Cathal to tell them who is the god that he worships. He says the Sun and the Moon and the Wind and others. The conversation continues thus…

Spirits — *Hast thou heard of Keithoir?*
Cathal — *No.*
Spirits — *He is the god of the green world. He dreams, and his dreams are Springtide and Summertime and Appletide. When he sleeps without dream there is winter.*
Cathal — *Have you no other god but this earth-god?*
Spirits — *Keithoir is our god. We know no other.*

From these few short passages regarding Keithoir it is clear that he is an important Faery god of the earth energies and of the plants and animals. The earlier reference to him becoming blind and weary may be because of the weakening of the powers of Nature due to the ever-encroaching and dominating presence of humankind. But he is still here, he has not disappeared completely, and we can still contact him and work with him in learning more Faery lore of the secrets and energies of the earth itself.

The weaver goddess Orchil is similarly a full-blooded Faery goddess who does not appear in any mythologies of the human world. It is true there are many weaver goddesses scattered across the mythologies of many people, but none bear the name Orchil. The fact that she is subterranean implies that she not only controls the fate and destiny of humankind, and, it would seem, the fate and destiny of the Faery gods themselves, but she is also connected with the very basic and fundamental powers and energies of the earth. Her control of Angus Ogue and her power over the seasons as displayed in this short tale confirms this. She also has great and ancient knowledge, for out of all of these old and powerful Celtic and Faery gods – Keithoir, Manannan, Hesus and Angus Ogue himself – she is the only one who understands fully what is going on and what she needs to do to rejuvenate the earth energies.

She is mentioned in a passage from the tale of *Ula and Urla*, to be found in *The Sin-Eater*, which says,

> *"Orchil, the dim goddess who is under the brown earth, in a vast cavern, where she weaves at two looms. With one hand she weaves life upward through the grass; with the other she weaves death downward through the mould; and the sound of the weaving is Eternity, and the name of it in the green world is Time. And, through all, Orchil weaves the weft of Eternal Beauty, that passeth not, though its soul is Change."*

Note the use of the word 'beauty', a synonym for the Realm of Faery, as noted earlier. Another reference, this one in Fiona's second book *The Mountain Lovers*, has this:

> *"High and low, the innumerous hum of insects vibrated on the air. Thus may the hum of the wheeling world be heard at Keithoir, who dreams in the hollow of a green hill unknown of man: or of the ancient goddess Orchil, who, blind and dumb, works in silence at the heart of Earth at her loom Change, with the thridding shuttles Life and Death: or of Manannan, who sleeps under the green wave, hearing only the sigh of the past, the moan of the passing, the rune of what is to come."*

The tale of *The Awakening of Angus Òg* given above ends with the following postscript:

> *"And that is why, when Orchil weaves dumbly in the dark: and Keithoir is blind, and dreams among remote hills and by unfrequented shores: and Manannan lies heavy with deep sleep, with the oceans of the world like moving shadows above him: and Hesus is grown white and hoar with the frost of waning stars and weary with the burden of new worlds — that is why Angus Ogue, the youthful god, is more ancient than they, and is for ever young. Their period is set. Oblivion is on the march against their immemorial time. But in the heart of Angus Ogue blooms the Rose of Youth, whose beauty is everlasting. Yea, Time is the name of that rose, and Eternity the beauty and fragrance thereof."*

This clearly reveals the great importance of the god Angus Ogue. He is from Faery and is important to the Faeries. He appears in all four branches of Celtic mythology. He is one of the few gods who actively goes out of his way to help humans. He fell in love with a mortal human woman. There are countless folk-tales concerning him and his adventures. Fiona is making it obvious that if you wish to start a relationship with any of the Faery gods or goddesses he should be your first choice.

However I would contend that the most important of the Faery gods that Fiona revealed to us is Dalua, but he is one you definitely do not want to seek out.

This god appears in several of Fiona's works under his own name and under titles such as Master of Illusion, the Amadan-Dhu (the Black Fool), the Secret Fool, the Accursed of the Everlasting Ones, God of Enchantment, and the Haughty Father. He is said to be the dark brother of Angus Ogue and his wife is the deadly Bean-Nimhir (The Serpent Woman) who is herself the dark aspect of St. Brigid. Fiona's first story specifically about Dalua is entitled simply *Dalua* and appeared in *The Dominion of Dreams*. This story opens with the following poem:

> *I have heard you calling, Dalua*
> > *Dalua!*
> *I have heard you on the hill,*
> *By the pool-side still,*
> *Where the lapwings shrill*
> > *Dalua … Dalua … Dalua!*
>
> *What is it you call, Dalua,*
> > *Dalua!*
> *When the rains fall,*
> *When the mists crawl*
> > *Dalua … Dalua … Dalua!*
>
> *I am the Fool, Dalua,*
> > *Dalua!*
> *When men hear me, their eyes*
> *Darken: the shadow in the skies*
> *Droops: and the keening-woman cries*
> > *DALUA … DALUA … DALUA!*

The story then introduces all the main themes and symbols of Dalua: the curlew, madness, illusions and shadows, the playing of hypnotic music, and his touch that brings madness or death. But the most important aspect is that very often, as in this tale, Dalua brings death or madness for no obvious reason. Dan Macara, the main character of the tale, has done nothing wrong, is not an evil man, and as far as we know has never done anything to slight Dalua, yet he becomes the victim of an unprovoked attack by the Dark Fool that leaves Dan physically injured and permanently mad. Why? It is all rather pointless as it stands. This is the way of Dalua. He is not responsible for his actions and he has no feelings for them, good or bad. He does what he has to do and moves on. The warning is that Dalua can appear to anyone, anywhere and at any time, and it is impossible to predict the outcome of his visit.

In the same book, *The Dominion of Dreams*, there is a tale called *By the Yellow Moonrock* in which Dalua once again attacks an innocent person, a drunken piper called Rory McAlpine who in this case ends up dead. This story is similar to the first in that Rory, like Dan Macara, has done nothing to deserve such a horrible end but is the victim of an unprovoked attack.

The Birds of Emar, also from *The Dominion of Dreams*, is the most Faery of all Fiona's stories involving Dalua. At first it seems to be dealing with several identifiable gods from the Celtic tradition but as the tale unfolds it takes on a very different form and character from any other Celtic myth. The writing style is very unusual for Fiona with many short, abrupt sentences and none of the lengthy descriptive passages that are so much her signature. Events happen very quickly and there is so much shape-shifting and swapping of places between humans and Faeries and back again that it is difficult to follow exactly what is going on. It is clearly a story taken straight from the Faery mythology and, as such, makes for very peculiar reading. It is worth reading slowly and carefully, meditating on all the gods and goddesses, heroes and heroines mentioned, as well as visualising the various actions and episodes they are engaged in. There is much to be learned from this but it takes a lot of unravelling. In the tale she makes reference to someone she identifies only as 'the Haughty Father.' This is Dalua in his aspect of the dark side of Christ. He appears in this form again in one of Fiona's better-known poems, *Invocation of Peace,* that we shall examine in depth in Chapter Eleven.

Fiona says more on this Haughty Father aspect of Dalua in a piece entitled *The Hill-Tarn* from *The Silence of Amor*. The hill tarn, or pool, of the title is said to be in Ross-shire, northern Scotland, and in the essay she describes the seven mountains that surround it. Of one of these she says:

"It is called Maol Athair-Uaibhreach, the Hill of the Haughty Father: I know not why. 'The Haughty Father' is a Gaelic analogue for the Prince of Darkness — son of Saturn, as he is called in an old poem: 'God's Elder Brother,' as he is named in a legend that I have met or heard of once only — a legend that He was God of this world before 'Mac Greinne' (lit.: Son of the Sun) triumphed over him, and drove him out of the East and out of the South, leaving him only in the West and in the North two ancient forgotten cities of the moon, that in the West below the thunder of grey skies and that in the North under the last shaken auroras of the Pole."

Note that God only drove Dalua the Haughty Father out of half of the world, East and South, leaving him the West and North for his domain: coincidentally the areas of Europe where the Celts still live to this day, thus making another link between the Celtic people and the Faeries. Note yet again the reference to the Aurora Borealis and the North Pole.

In *Studies in Spiritual History of the Gael* there is a short essay entitled simply *A Dream* which is written in a very mystical style, so unusual for Fiona. It seems to be another version of the Faery creation legend but the important point is that in this version Dalua is already in existence and is witness to the whole of Creation unfolding. This clearly makes him not just ancient but literally timeless and by implication elevates him to the highest aspect of the original Godhead as already indicated in the excerpt in the paragraph above. Here is the essay in full.

I was on a vast, an illimitable plain, where the dark blue horizons were sharp as the edges of hills. It was the world, but there was nothing in the world. There was not a blade of grass nor the hum of an insect, nor the shadow of a bird's wing. The mountains had sunk like waves in the sea when there is no wind; the barren hills had become dust. Forests had become the fallen leaf; and the leaf had passed. I was aware of one who stood beside me, though that knowledge was of the spirit only; and my eyes were filled with the same nothingness as I beheld above and beneath and beyond. I would have thought I was in the last empty glens of Death, were it not for a strange and terrible sound that I took to be the voice of the wind coming out of nothing, travelling over nothingness and moving onward into nothing.

"There is only the wind," I said to myself in a whisper.

Then the voice of the dark Power beside me, whom in my heart I knew to be Dalua, the Master of Illusions, said: "Verily, this is your last illusion."

I answered: "It is the wind."

And the voice answered: "That is not the wind you hear, for the wind is dead. It is the empty, hollow echo of my laughter."

Then, suddenly, he who was beside me lifted up a small stone, smooth as a pebble of the sea. It was grey and flat, and yet to me had a terrible beauty because it was the last vestige of the life of the world.

The Presence beside me lifted up the stone and said: "It is the end."

And the horizons of the world came in upon me like a rippling shadow. And I leaned over darkness and saw swirling stars. These were gathered up like leaves blown from a tree, and in a moment their lights were quenched, and they were further from me than grains of sand blown on a whirlwind of a thousand years.

Then he, that terrible one, Master of Illusions, let fall the stone, and it sank into the abyss and fell immeasurably into the infinite. And under my feet the world was as a falling wave, and was not. And I fell, though without sound, without motion. And for years and years I fell below the dim waning of light; and for years and years I fell through universes of dusk; and for years and years and years I fell through the enclosing deeps of darkness. It was to me as though I fell for centuries, for aeons, for unimaginable time. I knew I had fallen beyond time, and that I inhabited eternity, where were neither height, nor depth, nor width, nor space.

But, suddenly, without sound, without motion, I stood steadfast upon a ledge. Before me, on that ledge of darkness become rock, I saw this stone which had been lifted from the world of which I was a shadow, after shadow itself had died away. And as I looked, this stone became fire and rose in flame. Then the flame was not. And when I looked the stone was water; and it was as a pool that did not overflow, a wave that did not rise or fall, a shaken mirror wherein nothing was troubled.

Then, as dew is gathered in silence, the water was without form or colour or motion. And the stone seemed to me like a handful of earth held idly in the poise of unseen worlds. What I thought was a green flame rose from it, and I saw that it had the greenness of grass, and had the mystery of life. The green herb passed as green grass in a drought; and I saw the waving of wings. And I saw shape upon shape, and image upon image, and symbol upon symbol. Then I saw a man and he, too, passed; and I saw a woman, and she, too, passed; and I saw a child, and the child passed. Then the stone was a Spirit. And it shone there like a lamp. And I fell backward through deeps of darkness, through unimaginable time.

And when I stood upon the world again it was like a glory. And I saw the stone lying at my feet.

And One said: "Do you not know me, brother?"

And I said: "Speak, Lord."

And Christ stooped and kissed me upon the brow.

Note that the dream starts with Dalua, the dark aspect of Christ, standing next to the narrator and talking with her but at the end of her timeless vision her companion has become the Christ of Light. Note also that Christ calls her 'brother' – so who is relating the story? Clearly not Fiona.

The Lynn of Dreams, a story from *The Winged Destiny*, centres on a character referred to only as 'John o' Dreams.' He is a master poet and wordsmith but he longs to find the source of all poetry, of all words, the true inspiration behind all verse and song. One day as he is dreaming on this he realises that Dalua is standing beside him. Dalua knows his desire and says he can take him to the pool that is the fount of all language. The poet goes with him until they reach a small pool and therein he sees more than he can possibly comprehend regarding poetry, songs, stories and language in all its many forms and manifestations.

As he gazes in wonder he is suddenly startled by the sound of a plover's cry – the plover, or curlew, is a symbol of Dalua. The pool vanishes and he is back where he first met Dalua. He asks what has happened and Dalua says he gave him a drink from the Lynn of Dreams, the pool of all words and inspiration. However from that moment forth the poet can no longer compose verse, make wise utterances or even deal with the simplicities of every day language. He had seen too much and could not cope with it. The story ends with, *"It was all gone: the master-touch, the secret art, the craft. He became an obscure stammerer. At the last he was dumb. And then his heart broke, and he died. But had not the Master of Illusions shown him his heart's desire, and made it his?"* This final sentence concerning Dalua granting the heart's desire that brings death with it is also the crux of Fiona's important play *The Immortal Hour*.

I discuss *The Immortal Hour* in depth in my book *The Little Book of the Great Enchantment* but it is worth quoting a few sections from the play dealing with Dalua. In one place we are told:

> *"On a quicken [the mountain ash tree], growing from mid-earth and hanging like a spar across the depths, Dalua sits: and sometimes through the dusk of immemorial congregated time, his laughter rings: and then he listens long, and when the echo swims up from the deeps he springs from crag to crag, for he is mad, and like a lost lamb crieth to his ewe, that ancient dreadful Mother of the Gods whom men call Fear. Even the high gods who laugh and mock the lonely Fairy Fool when in his mortal guise he haunts the earth, shrink from the Amadan Dhu when in their ways he moves, silent, unsmiling, wearing a dark star above his foam white brows and midnight eyes."*

This lets us know that Dalua walks with equal ease among humans and among the high gods of the Faeries. Fiona also points out a difference in his stature depending on where he is. When he walks among us he is known as the Fairy Fool and has no power in the Faery realm, for it is when he is here on earth that the Faery gods feel safe in their laughter and mockery of him. But when he is in their realm he becomes the Dark Fool and the powerful Faery gods grow silent and shrink from him. In legend and folklore we are often told that the things of this world are reversed in the Faery world. This is but another example of this reversal.

If Dalua is a mad, pathetic creature deserving pity in our world then it makes sense that in the realm of Faery he becomes a creature of power and stature that even the gods wish to avoid. However, as a further section in *The Immortal Hour* points out, he is unable to control his movements between one world and the other. He is tossed between them as some higher need determines. This theme of loss of control of location is brought up later in the play when Dalua realises he has suddenly been transferred from the Hebrides of Scotland to the gloomy Faery forest where the play opens. As we know, the Hebridean islands were important places to Fiona Macleod, Seumas Macleod and William Sharp, and according to the Faery volume *The Chronicles of the Sidhe*, a place where remnants of the Faeries still remain.

The specific link between Dalua and the Hebrides is made clear in a short essay Fiona called *When Dalua Was A Prince Of This World*. I give it in full here as it only appeared in one of the limited edition American printings of Fiona's works, *The Silence of Amor*, published by Thomas Mosher in 1902, that is not so easy to find these days.

> *When Dalua the King came to the Isles of the West, none but those who had hidden wisdom knew of it. No one saw him by day or by night: the wisest knew not whence he had come, or when or whither he would go. Dusk lay on whatsoever path he trod, and his feet were shod with silence. But after many days it was known to all that the Dark King was there, and all feared him.*
>
> *The days slid by, like wave on wave into an ebbing tide, and perhaps the King gave no sign: but one day he would give a sign: and that sign was a laughing that was heard somewhere, upon the lonely hills, or by desolate shores, or in the heart of him who heard. And whenever the King laughed, he who heard would go from his clan to join the King in the shadow.*
>
> *But sometimes Dalua the Dark King laughed in the unpeopled solitudes, only*

because of vain hopes and wild imaginings, for upon these he lives as well as upon the savours of death.

To-night, dreaming, I stood in a waste place, where the wind whistled in the grass, though I saw no leaf stir, no reed quiver. The wind passed, and the moon rose, and the wailing of plovers ceased. But Dalua neither heard me nor saw me, for was I not there as a phantom only, the phantom of a dream? There, in that unpeopled solitude, I knew that he went his secret way, for I heard a wild and lonely laughter in the night. Was it because of vain hopes and vain imaginings borne by that whistling wind out of bowed and broken hearts?

Answer, O heart, that so many imaginings have filled, so many hopes lifted.

Fiona wrote another poem dealing with Dalua called *The Lords Of Shadow* that gives us more useful symbolism.

Where the water whispers 'mid the shadowy
  rowan-trees
I have heard the Hidden People like the hum
  of swarming bees:
And when the moon has risen and the brown
  burn glisters grey
I have seen the Green Host marching in
  laughing disarray.

Dalua then must sure have blown a sudden
  magic air
Or with the mystic dew sealed my eyes
  from seeing fair:
For the great Lords of Shadow who tread the
  deeps of night
Are no frail puny folk who move in dread of
  mortal sight.

For sure Dalua laughed alow, Dalua the fairy
  Fool,
When with his wildfire eyes he saw me 'neath
  the rowan-shadowed pool:
His touch can make the chords of life a bitter
  jangling tune,
The false glows true, the true glows false,
  beneath his moontide rune.

The laughter of the Hidden Host is terrible to
  hear,
The Hounds of Death would harry me at
  lifting of a spear:
Mayhap Dalua made for me the hum of
  swarming bees
And sealed my eyes with dew beneath the
  shadowy rowan-trees.

I would suggest that if you wish to make contact with or learn more of the nature of the Faery gods and goddesses that you concentrate first on Angus and then perhaps move on to Orchil and Keithoir.

Dalua is there. He cannot be ignored. But he is not a contact to be encouraged or sought after. I have given more information on him in *The Little Book of the Great Enchantment* which I would advise you to study carefully. He is a necessary force and his sombre task is one that is repeated constantly throughout the Green World of Nature in which we all live. Being aware of him and of his task is as essential as being aware of Angus Ogue and his sympathetic leanings towards humans. But resist the temptation to get too close.

Chapter Seven

THE MYTHOLOGY OF FAERY

Truly we are all one. It is a common tongue we speak, though the wave has its own whisper, and the wind its own sigh, and the lip of man its word and the heart of woman its silence.

ALL PEOPLES AND CULTURES of this world have a mythology; the tales, songs, poems and beliefs that explain how things came into being, who the gods and goddesses are, why the ways of the world are mysterious and sometimes dangerous and so forth. Early mythologies are often hopelessly entangled with the factual history of the people and this can make separating fact from fiction a difficult task for the historian. However, to the ancient ones who in their wisdom created each and every mythology, these stories, songs and poems *were their factual history*. It is we modern humans in our analytical and dissecting world who have reclassified some of these early histories as 'mythology.' This is usually done for no other reason than the modern scientific mind finds many of the early histories of indigenous people to be so fantastic and impossible to believe that they cannot be accepted as historical fact by the modern recorder and researcher. They are therefore reclassified as mythology – meaning they are worthy of study but not to be taken literally. For the mythologist there should be no such separation between fact and fiction, history and mythology. It is all one, it is all valid.

The Faeries are not of this world but they too have their own personal history and mythology. Just as the stories of human mythology cross over from our world into the nebulous world of the Faeries, so too does Faery mythology straddle the gap between their world and ours. It is these points of contact between Faery and human mythology that are of interest to us both. Our world has many mythologies because of our great diversity of peoples and cultures. These different mythologies all start with their own version of the Creation Myth; who or what created the world and all it contains, and how things came to be the way we see them today. Faery mythology is no different. It has its own Creation Myth, a myth that contains a great deal of valuable lore for not only the Faeries but for humans as well. Fiona Macleod recounted this story within the tale *Orpheus and Oisin* that can be found in the collection of her tales called *The Winged Destiny*.

The story concerns a character called *Faruane*. This is an anglicized spelling of two words from the Gaelic language, 'Fear-uaine', which translates as *green man*. The Green Man is a figure that has found his way into human mythology and folklore but his origins seem to be from the Faery Creation Myth, as the following story relates.

"Faruane lived in the old ancient days in a great oak, and had so lived for generations. He did nothing but watch the clouds sail above the branches and the shadows glide between the tree-boles, and live on sunlight and dew. Then one day, as he was walking lightly on the moss, he saw another world come lightly into the old untroubled world, and that 'world' was a woman. She was young as Niamh the undying, and beautiful as Emer the fair, and bewitching as Liban of the spells; and Faruane grew weary of his calm immortal dream, and longed unwittingly for sorrow and death, for he did not know these companions of the soul, nor even that he longed, nor could he know that a soul was other than a perishable thing of the earth as he himself was. So he moved softly on the sun-warmed dusk of the branches and came upon the girl (whose name was Mo-an) among the fern where she stood like a fawn with wide eyes. He was too beautiful for her to fear, and too beautiful for her not to love, and although Mo-an knew that to give herself in love to a wood-spirit was to live three years in a dream and then die in body and to go away in soul, she put from her all desire of the things she knew and let Faruane kiss her on the lips and take her hand and lead her into the green glades, to be forgotten, beyond the murmuring forest, save in a song that lived like a breath of remembered passion in the gloamings of a thousand years.

But for three years Faruane and Mo-an knew the Spring rapture and the Summer joy and the Autumn peace and the Winter sleep of the children of earth. She remembered nothing, for her soul was filled with beauty; and she desired nothing, for her mind was hushed with dreams and honeyed with content.

But when she died, which was as a child falling asleep in a shadowy place of moss and rustling leaves, Faruane faded from the light, and his death was as a sunbeam passing from a green branch; for he had seen her soul stoop and kiss him and go away to its own place, where he could not follow. But they had daughters, and these lived to the fullness of the green hour, which is calm and unaging through many generations of our fevered mortal day. They in turn bore children to other sons of the greenness, the semblance of Mo-an, but in all else of the seed of Faruane; so that they are like the offspring of the clan of men, but fear them and love them not, and may not dwell with them or near them, nor wed with them. But they love the shadows of leaves, and the sun ripens them as fruit, and they are forgotten, and have no dreams but the dream that is their life."

There are clear similarities between this tale and the biblical story of the Garden of Eden – they are both set in a garden or forest; when the story starts there is only a man present but he is soon joined by a woman; they know nothing of death or decay; eventually the man's joint experiences with the woman lead him to experience and realise much more of the world than he had ever known before; this knowledge brings with it an understanding that he can never return to his previous, naïve state of being; they have children who then go on to populate the world.

Despite these similarities there are many major differences between the biblical version and the Faery version, the most obvious being that God is not involved in the Faery version. Nor is the concept of sin and punishment introduced in the Faery version as it is in the biblical version where Adam, Eve and the serpent are all punished for Adam's disobedience of God's decree not to partake of the fruit of a particular tree.

Note that the tale opens with *"Faruane lived in the old ancient days"*. There is no attempt to explain how he got there, who created him or anything else that lived in the forest with him. All we are told is that this happened a very long time ago. This is in keeping not only with the Faery tradition but also the Celtic tradition, where to put it simply, Time just is. There is no beginning and no future. All that was, is, or ever shall be, is right here, right now. This same reasoning optimistically implies that everything that is here now will always be here, but that is a subject for another book, I think.

We are informed that Faruane lived *"in a great oak and had so lived for generations."* Here is another crossover between Faery and Celtic symbolism. Superficially the fact he lived in an oak tree is irrelevant. All we need to know is that he lived in a tree, not a hut or shelter or cave. So why specifically mention the oak tree?

In the ancient Celtic alphabet known as 'Ogham' the name of each letter is also the name of a tree. This is still the case with the names of the letters in the modern Gaelic language. However this simple alphabet is also the basis for a magical system that has many layers of meaning and symbolism. For the moment suffice to say that the oak tree symbolizes the High King. To the Celtic people the High King was a spiritual ruler rather than a dynastic or political ruler. By connecting Faruane with the oak and thereby with the spiritual High King we are made aware that he is of more importance than we may at first have realised. An important point to note is that in several of her writings Fiona describes Faery beings that live inside trees. The subject of this tale is clearly Faery and not Celtic.

Next we are told that this important, solitary individual *"did nothing but watch the clouds sail above the branches and the shadows glide between the tree-boles, and live on sunlight and dew."* In other words his life was spent in a state of inaction. He did not actually *do* anything. He did not even have to hunt or gather food. Sunshine fell on him and dew gathered on him and these kept him alive. All he did was pass time simply by being alive. Creation, as we would understand it, was still only in potential; action had not yet come into his world.

When action does eventually come into his world it does not stop. This is another difference between Faery Creation and biblical Creation. According to the Bible story, once God had spent six days creating everything he rested, and basically Creation was finished. In the Faery tradition, once action was no longer a mere potential but became actual, it carried on and still is carrying on. In other words, Creation is an on-going process. It always will be, it will have no end: and this fits in well with the Faery and Celtic concept of time, as defined above.

The narrative then goes on to tell us *"Then one day, as he was walking lightly on the moss, he saw another world come lightly into the old untroubled world, and that 'world' was a woman."* This is an odd turn of phrase to our mind – he saw another world come into his and that this world was a woman. However until that point *he* had been all that there was in the world. He literally was his own world. The fact he now saw for the first time another being would indeed seem to him that another entire world was encroaching on his. Note also that the tale comments that until that time his old world had been *"untroubled"*, implying that he intuitively realised things were about to change. Who this woman was, who created her, where she came from or how she got there is never explained, she just is, as Faruane just is.

The next sentence is very important. *"Faruane grew weary of his calm immortal dream, and longed unwittingly for sorrow and death, for he did not know these companions of the soul, nor even that he longed, nor could he know that a soul was other than a perishable thing of the earth as he himself was."*

The coming of this woman had started to change the static, inert world that he had known up until now. He started to experience longing, a new thing for him. But the longing he had was one of sorrow. He did not feel joy at seeing another being. He did not feel optimism that now his life would be fuller and more enriching. He felt an unwitting longing for sorrow and death. Until this point both of these concepts or states were unknown to him. He had neither knowledge nor experience of either of them, but something in him stirred and awakened at the sight of this woman and the result was one of sorrow.

Here is another major difference between the Faery Creation Myth and the biblical Eden story. In the biblical version Adam had been longing for a companion; God created a woman, and Adam and the woman were both filled with joy. Faruane will have to wait a while before he experiences joy. Fiona used joy and sorrow and their interplay and interactions with each other over and over again in her stories, essays, tales and plays. It is the crux of the Faery Tradition and will be pointed out repeatedly when appropriate throughout this book. For the moment, it is sufficient to take note that sorrow and joy have now come into the world of Faery and that it was sorrow that came first.

The rest of this section shows that up until now he had been in a completely neutral state and did not know that he had longing or that longing could even exist, and that he had no concept of Self. He was unaware of his own soul, his own immortality. The appearance of this woman brought so many new and important things to Faruane that it is now clear why he called her a "world." She brought with her a world of change just by being there. They have not even started to interact act this stage; no words have been exchanged, no physical contact. This shows very dramatically how powerful a mere image can be and how so many new thoughts, ideas and emotions can be stimulated by simply looking upon a visual image. This is the crux of much magical work and helps to explain why so many occult groups, secret societies and even indigenous peoples keep their sacred and magical images hidden from the profane.

The next part of the narrative now tells us, indirectly, that Mo-an has come from the human world. It says *"Mo-an knew that to give herself in love to a wood-spirit was to live three years in a dream and then die in body and to go away in soul, she put from her all desire of the things she knew and let Faruane kiss her on the lips and take her hand and lead her into the green glades, to be forgotten, beyond the murmuring forest, save in a song that lived like a breath of remembered passion in the gloamings of a thousand years."* We can infer from several things here that she was human. First, she knew that Faruane was a wood-spirit, and therefore different from her in that he was not human. Second, she had a belief that to give herself to this non-human wood-spirit would bring about her own death. Other people must have told her that such was the case and that there was a taboo on making such a mixed-blood union. This tells us she came from a place where she was not alone, unlike Faruane in his solitary forest. She also knew that she could die physically and that she had a soul, two concepts unknown and undreamt of by Faruane. When she gave herself totally to Faruane she knew that she would forever lose contact with her fellow humans and that they would forget her, other than as a character in an old folksong. All these things point to Mo-an being human and from a time in human evolution when people knew of wood-spirits, or the Faeries, and believed it was wise to stay away from them.

Despite this she went to him gladly and voluntarily, knowing that her actions would bring about her own death. She did this because she knew her actions would give Faruane the fullest experience of the passion that is brought with joy and sorrow, and that in so doing he would experience his own soul. Her self-sacrificing actions display the highest spiritual, moral and ethical values that a human can hold. Again this positive depiction of Mo-an and her selfless actions is a total reversal of the image given to Eve in the biblical story, despite the fact that her actions were in essence the same as Mo-an's.

The next short paragraph tells us that an awareness of the passing of time had now been brought to the Realm of Faery, when the two lovers noted the changing of the seasons for a period of three years. This was a major change in the Realm of Faery. Compare this with the discussion of *The Chronicles of the Sidhe* in Chapter Four where the Faeries break contact with the human world and reject our understanding of time by declaring that the tides of the sea will no longer flow in the Realm of Faery. The concept of the steady passing of time seems to be a concept the Faeries can well do without.

Mo-an's prediction of her death after three years came true. The narrative says *"But when she died, which was as a child falling asleep in a shadowy place of moss and rustling leaves, Faruane faded from the light, and his death was as a sunbeam passing from a green branch; for he had seen her soul stoop and kiss him and go away to its own place, where he could not follow."* Note that the description of her passing is very gentle and beautiful, not a frightening, sorrowful or upsetting thing at all. Her death though brought with it a change of state for Faruane, who passed on to a different afterlife or Otherworld than Mo-an did. Hers was a place where he could not follow, and this reveals that there is more than one Otherworld and that intercourse between them may not always be possible. This Faery concept of there being more than one world of non-physical being is important and must be kept in mind by those of us in our world who attempt communication with the Realm of Faery. There is a real danger of getting lost and many folk-songs and folk-tales from all over the planet have been warning us of this for centuries. Take note.

Next we are told that they had daughters, presumably three, one for each year they were together, and they in turn had offspring. The narrative says of this *"They in turn bore children to other sons of the greenness, the semblance of Mo-an, but in all else of the seed of Faruane; so that they are like the offspring of the clan of men, but fear them and love them not, and may not dwell with them or near them, nor wed with them. But they love the shadows of leaves, and the sun ripens them as fruit, and they are forgotten, and have no dreams but the dream that is their life."*

So these half-human, half-Faery descendents of the original couple bore children to *"other sons of the greenness"* (remember Faruane means the 'green man') or, in other words, to the Faeries, not humans, and thereby kept the mixed blood alive in the Realm of Faery. These mixed blood offspring look more human, like Mo-an, than they do Faery, but nonetheless are more Faery in spirit and nature than their looks imply. As mentioned earlier in this book Fiona hinted at two of her human acquaintances, Edith Wingate Rinder and Catherine Janvier, as being of mixed Faery-human blood.

The wording of this last section is very important. We are clearly told that despite the fact these new-style Faeries look like the offspring of humans and have human blood in their veins, they may not have any contact with us and, indeed, actually fear us. But note in particular the narrative says they *"may not"* have any contact with humans. This careful wording denotes that there is a formal prohibition amongst Faeries that they are not allowed to have such intercourse. It is not a matter of personal choice or prejudice; they *may not* do such a thing. However despite this prohibition we know from the revelations of Fiona Macleod and others that such Faery-human mating has taken place over the generations. In *Carmina Gadelica* there are many warnings, particularly between runes number 507 and 520, of the grave dangers of taking a Faery lover and of having children by this lover. It was clearly a situation that was much on the minds of the people, and one they knew, like the Faeries knew, should not be permitted.

This brings a final and very interesting similarity with the Bible where in Genesis Chapter 4 we are told: *"The Nephilim were in the earth in those days, and also after that, when the sons of God came unto the daughters of men, and they bore children to them: the same were the mighty men that were of old, the men of renown."* It has long been argued who or what the Nephilim were but all agree that they were not human, and God put a prohibition on the Nephilim having any further sexual contact with human women. Here the Bible and the Faery Creation Myth are in agreement. The mixing of human and non-human blood is taboo.

The next tale we should look at from the mythology of Faery is, in a sense, a conclusion to the story of Faruane. It explains how humans can have the Deep Knowledge of the Realm of Faery despite the fact the Faeries are forbidden from having relationships with us. It also opens up a whole new area of speculation and research for those interested in the more mystical and magical aspects of Christ's life and teachings.

Fiona revealed this important Faery myth in a story she called *How Deep Knowledge Came to the Child Jesus*. It forms the last part of the Prologue to *The Washer of the Ford* and is dedicated to Kathia who was Fiona's friend Catherine Janvier, mentioned above as perhaps being of Faery blood. Later in 1908, Thomas B. Mosher, one of Fiona's American publishers, reprinted it in the little volume *Three Legends of the Christ Child*. It should be noted here that when Fiona used the word 'Deep,' as in the title of this story, it was a euphemism for Faery. Hence the Deep Knowledge is the knowledge of the Faeries and the Deep Peace (discussed in Chapter Eleven) is the peace of the Faeries. This story is quite remarkable as it makes clear that when the Christ came to this world he had no knowledge of the Green World or the Realm of Faery until an ancient Faery king revealed it to him. This is hardly accepted Christian doctrine but this in itself reveals that the Faeries do have knowledge of the Christ but are not influenced or affected by the doctrine, dogma and often senseless debate that have mired his teachings by the religious zealots of this world. The tale is as follows.

How Deep Knowledge Came to the Child Jesus

Everywhere we see the life of Man in subservient union with the life of Nature; never, in a word, by a sun beset by tributary stars, but as one planet among the innumerous concourse of the sky, nurtured, it may be, by light from other luminaries and other spheres than we know of. That we are intimately at one with Nature is a cosmic truth we are all slowly approaching.

It is not only the dog, it is not only the wild beast and the wood-dove, that are our close kindred, but the green tree and the green grass, the blue wave and the flowing wind, the flower of day and the granite peak of an aeon.

We are woven in one loom, and the Weaver thrids our being with the sweet influences, not only of the Pleiades, but of the living world of which each is no more than a multi-coloured thread: as, in turn, He thrids the wandering wind with the inarticulate cry, the yearning, the passion, the pain of that bitter clan, the Human.

Truly we are all one. It is a common tongue we speak, though the wave has its own whisper, and the wind its own sigh, and the lip of man its word and the heart of woman its silence.

Legend

Long, long ago a desert king, old and blind, but dowered with ancestral wisdom beyond all men that have lived, heard that the Son of God was born among men. He rose from his place, and on the eve of the third day he came to where Jesus sat among the gifts brought by the wise men of the East. The little lad sat in Mary's lap, beneath a tree filled with quiet light; and while the folk of Bethlehem came and went He was only a child as other children are. But when the desert king drew near, the child's eyes deepened with knowledge.

"What is it, my little son?" said Mary the Virgin.

"Sure, mother dear," said Jesus, who had never yet spoken a word, "it is Deep Knowledge that is coming to me."

"And what will that be, O my Wonder and Glory?"

"That which will come in at the door before you speak to me again."

Even as the child spoke, an old blind man entered and bowed his head. "Come near, O tired old man," said Mary that had borne a son to Joseph, but whose womb knew him not. With that the tears fell into the old man's beard.

"Sorrow of sorrows," he said, "but that will be the voice of the Queen of Heaven!"

But Jesus said to his mother, "Take up the tears and throw them into the dark night."

And Mary did so: and lo! upon the wilderness, where no light was, and on the dark wave, where seamen toil without hope, clusters of stars rayed downwards in a white peace. Thereupon the old king of the desert said: "Heal me, O King of the Elements." And Jesus healed him. His sight was upon him again, and his grey ancientness was green youth once more.

"I have come with Deep Knowledge," he said.

"Ay, sure, I am for knowing that," said the King of the Elements, that was a little child.

"Well, if you will be knowing that, you can tell me who is at my right side?"

"It is my elder brother, the Wind."

"And what colour will the Wind be?"

"Now blue as Hope, now green as Compassion."

"And who is on my left?"

"The Shadow of Life."

"And what colour will the Shadow be?"

"That which is woven out of the bowels of the earth and out of the belly of the sea."

"Truly, thou art the King of the Elements. I am bringing you a great gift, I am: I have come with Deep Knowledge." And with that the old blind man, whose eyes were now as stars, and whose youth was a green garland about him, chanted nine runes.

The first rune was the Rune of the Four Winds.

The second rune was the Rune of the Deep Seas.

The third rune was the Rune of the Lochs and Rivers and Rains and Dews and the many Waters.

The fourth rune was the Rune of the Green Trees and of all things that grow.

The fifth rune was the Rune of Man and Bird and Beast, and of everything that lives and moves, in the air, on the earth, and in the sea: all that is seen of man, and all that is unseen of man.

The sixth rune was the Rune of Birth, from the spawn on the wave to the Passion of Woman.

The seventh rune was the Rune of Death, from the quenching of a gnat to the fading of the stars.

The eighth rune was the Rune of the Soul that dieth not, and the Spirit that is.

The ninth rune was the Rune of the Mud, and the Dross and the Slime of Evil — that is the Garden of God wherein He walks with sunlight streaming from the palms of his hands and with stars springing beneath his feet.

Then when he had done the old man said: "I have brought you Deep Knowledge."

But at that Jesus the child said: "All this I heard on my way hither."

The old desert king bowed his head. Then he took a blade of grass and played upon it. It was a strange wild air that he played.

"Iosa Mac Dhé, tell the woman what song <u>that</u> is," cried the desert king.

"It is the speech of the Wind that is my Brother," cried the Child, clapping his hands for joy.

"And what will this be?" And the old man took a green leaf, and played a lovely whispering song.

"It is the speech of the leaves," cried Jesus the little lad, laughing now.

And thereafter the desert king played upon a handful of dust, and upon a drop of water, and upon a flame of fire; and the Child laughed for the knowing and the joy. Then he gave the secret speech of the singing bird, and the barking fox, and the howling wolf, and the bleating sheep: of all and every created kind.

"O King of the Elements," he said then, "for sure you know much; but now I have made you to know the secret things of the green Earth that is Mother of you and of Mary too."

But while Jesus pondered that one mystery the old man was gone: and when he got to his people, they put him alive into a hollow of the earth and covered him up, because of his shining eyes, and the green youth that was about him as a garland.

And when Christ was nailed upon the Cross, Deep Knowledge went back into the green world, and passed into the grass and the sap in trees, and the flowing wind, and the dust that swirls and is gone.

The opening section of the legend contains a good deal of useful information. First it is important to note that the person who brought Christ the Deep Knowledge is described as *"a desert king."* The title of king makes it clear he is a person of some importance but the use of the word desert lets us know that he comes from a place where the growing powers of the Green World are greatly restricted. Second, it may seem from the narrative that this desert king broke the Faery prohibition on having contact with humans but his sole contact was with Jesus Christ who, according to some esoteric teachings, was part Faery and, even if this was not the case, he was more a Son of God than a Son of Man.

When the king arrived in Bethlehem, Christ had already been born and of him the narrative says *"the folk of Bethlehem came and went* (and) *He was only a child as other children are"* which tells us that the ordinary people of the city, i.e. you and I, could not see Christ as he truly was. To them he was just another human baby. Then *"when the desert king drew near, the child's eyes deepened with knowledge."* He sensed someone other than one of the ordinary folk was approaching. Note that his eyes deepened with knowledge, not Deep Knowledge. This is important. Mary does not sense anything out of the ordinary is happening and Jesus explains, *"it is Deep Knowledge that is coming to me."* He did not say it was a man or a king that approached, but what that king held and represented that came near – Deep Knowledge. This is the same as when Faruane in the previous Faery myth called Mo-an 'a world.' The desert king is the physical embodiment of that Deep Knowledge. The story tells us that the Three Wise Men had already given the baby Jesus their gifts of the treasures of this world. Now the fourth 'wise man' was giving him the gift of knowledge, a fourth and much more precious gift. But it was not the knowledge of everyday things that he brought; Christ already had that. Instead he was given Deep Knowledge – the knowledge of the Faeries – a different thing altogether and something that was unknown to him and he did not yet possess.

When the desert king entered, Mary said *"Come near, O tired old man."* She did not have the intuition that her son did, and only saw an old blind man, not recognizing that he was a king. Since leaving his own world, the Realm of Faery, he had taken on the appearance of an ordinary man of our world. Upon hearing Mary's voice the king made his first statement. *"Sorrow of sorrows,"* he said, *"but that will be the voice of the Queen of Heaven!"* So, like Faruane in the Creation Myth, the first utterance that came from this keeper of Deep Knowledge was an expression of sorrow. Again, as in Faruane's case, this seems contradictory. When Faruane saw a woman approaching, his first companion, he felt sorrow, not joy. So too in this tale the powerful, all-knowing Faery king expressed not only sorrow but 'sorrow of sorrows' when he recognized the Queen of Heaven by her voice. By our understanding and way of doing things an expression of joy and rapture would be expected at such a realisation. But no, once again sorrow comes first. We shall examine both sorrow and joy in depth later. For the time being note that the king's physical expression of his sorrow, the tears that fell into his beard, were turned into the stars in the firmament. In other words they became guiding lights that bring hope and peace to everyone everywhere. His personal Faery sorrow had become a joy for all of humankind.

Next he displayed that he was incapable of healing himself of his blindness despite his Deep Knowledge. The narrative says, *"the old king of the desert said: "Heal me, O King of the Elements." And Jesus healed him. His sight was upon him again, and his grey ancientness was green youth once more."* Note that as well as restoring the king's physical sight Christ also transferred the old man back to his original Faery state. This is a good example of how we can learn so much from the Faeries but there are occasions when they need our help in practical ways. Even a king of the Faeries was unable to perform the rejuvenation that Christ did.

Once the healing had restored balance there followed a session of questions and answers meant to test each other's knowledge. The desert king started by asking Christ,

"…can (you) tell me who is at my right side?"

"It is my elder brother, the Wind."

"And what colour will the Wind be?"

"Now blue as Hope, now green as Compassion."

"And who is on my left?"

"The Shadow of Life."

"And what colour will the Shadow be?"

"That which is woven out of the bowels of the earth and out of the belly of the sea."

This formalized system of testing knowledge by a series of cryptic questions and answers is found frequently in the old Celtic legends. It is also the crucial part of attaining the Grail according to the Grail Mythology, and several of the stories and runes from *Carmina Gadelica* also demonstrate how such interplay of words can be used to force a Faery to leave your presence. The above section shows that such ritualized testing of knowledge, ability and worth is a practice used similarly by the Faeries. Anyone who is interested in Faery communication should take note of this.

In this short interchange the questions are straightforward enough but the answers are puzzling. Fiona makes frequent mention of the wind, and especially coloured winds, throughout her writings, and we shall examine these in detail later; but why did Christ call the Wind his elder brother? Note that he named specific colours for this Wind but when asked what colour is the Shadow of Life he did not name colours but rather said where you will find its colours, *"the bowels of the earth and the belly of the sea."*

The answers that Christ gave were clearly the right ones because the king then said, *"Truly, thou art the King of the Elements. I am bringing you a great gift, I am: I have come with Deep Knowledge." And with that the old blind man, whose eyes were now as stars, and whose youth was a green garland about him, chanted nine runes.*

The first rune was the Rune of the Four Winds.

The second rune was the Rune of the Deep Seas.

The third rune was the Rune of the Lochs and Rivers and Rains and Dews and the many Waters.

The fourth rune was the Rune of the Green Trees and of all things that grow.

The fifth rune was the Rune of Man and Bird and Beast, and of everything that lives and moves, in the air, on the earth, and in the sea: all that is seen of man, and all that is unseen of man.

The sixth rune was the Rune of Birth, from the spawn on the wave to the Passion of Woman.

The seventh rune was the Rune of Death, from the quenching of a gnat to the fading of the stars.

The eighth rune was the Rune of the Soul that dieth not, and the Spirit that is.

The ninth rune was the Rune of the Mud, and the Dross and the Slime of Evil — that is the Garden of God wherein He walks with sunlight streaming from the palms of his hands and with stars springing beneath his feet."

The first statement the king made acknowledged that Christ's answers entitled him to be known as the King of the Elements, the king of the human realm, but his answers did not display any understanding of the Deep Knowledge of Faery, so the Faery king then proceeded to give him this Deep Knowledge. Note the description of the Faery king at this stage; he had been blind but now his eyes were like stars and his youth had returned to him. In a sense he is living backwards, getting younger as time progresses. This is a common theme in many stories of the Faeries and indicates yet again that things in the Realm of Faery are not as they are in our little world, especially the apparent passing of time, as has already been discussed. It also shows that the passing on of the Deep Knowledge is a liberating and invigorating experience for the Faery king.

The Deep Knowledge that he passed on was in the form of nine runes (prayers or sayings) that cover every aspect of life in our world.

Unfortunately we are not told exactly what these runes say but the fact they have been revealed to Christ means that they have been brought into our realm and can be obtained by magical work in the Realm of Faery and also through a mystical experience of Christ.

This is an important point for many reasons. It tells us that the Faeries see in this particular case the value of studying the deeper meanings of the teachings of Christ. Fiona pointed this out over and over again by her numerous stories, commentaries and anecdotes concerning St. Columba. Even a casual look at the life of this early saint shows that he straddled the line between Christianity and the pre-Christian Faery tradition. Fiona, however, was clearly no great admirer of the institutionalised church of the Victorian era, as several of her essays reveal. But the early teachings and practices of the Celtic church were not as distorted and twisted by the small minds of men as they are today, and these early teachings and lives of the early Celtic saints still hold much of value for students of Faery lore and magic.

I commented above that the different winds were important to Fiona. Note that the first rune of the Deep Knowledge given out by the Faery king is the Rune of the Four Winds. There is not much more to say regarding these particular runes without knowing them word for word. Fortunately for us Fiona gave out plenty of other runes throughout her voluminous writings and we shall take a detailed look at some of these in Chapter Eight. For the moment, consider the imagery contained in the ninth rune. This evil, slimy, dirty place is the opposite of what we would expect of God's garden. This again shows how very differently things are seen and understood in Faery and it is crucial to keep this in mind.

After he had delivered his nine runes the Faery king told him,
"I have brought you Deep Knowledge."
But at that Jesus the child said: "All this I heard on my way hither."
The old desert king bowed his head. Then he took a blade of grass and played upon it. It was a strange wild air that he played.
"Iosa Mac Dhé, tell the woman what song that is," cried the desert king.
"It is the speech of the Wind that is my Brother," cried the Child, clapping his hands for joy.
"And what will this be?" And the old man took a green leaf, and played a lovely whispering song.
"It is the speech of the leaves," cried Jesus the little lad, laughing now.
And thereafter the desert king played upon a handful of dust, and upon a drop of

water, and upon a flame of fire; and the Child laughed for the knowing and the joy. Then he gave the secret speech of the singing bird, and the barking fox, and the howling wolf, and the bleating sheep: of all and every created kind.

Christ's response to being given the Deep Knowledge contained within the nine runes was a dismissive comment that he had learned all this stuff on his way into incarnation. The Faery king does not speak or comment on this rather rude dismissal of his precious gift but lets the voices of the Green World take over. We are told that he took a simple blade of grass and played a strange, wild music on it. The exact way he did this is not revealed, but it does not matter; the important point is that it was the voice of the grass, not the voice of the king, which now imparted further Deep Knowledge.

When he had stopped playing he tested Jesus ('Iosa Mac Dhé' is the Gaelic for 'Jesus Son of God') to see if he understood the voice of the grass, but note that the Faery king told Jesus to give his answer to Mary. So far in the story she has not played an active part in the events at all but this section implies that she had been listening to the whole conversation and taking note of what the Deep Knowledge meant. This is important. The Deep Knowledge of Faery, brought directly to Jesus Christ by a king of the Faeries, is meant for all, not just the Son of God, not just the 'high and mighty,' but all of humankind. Christ tells his mother that the music made upon the grass is the speech of the wind and, once again, he called the wind his Brother. The following revelations of the Deep Knowledge were through the speech of the leaves, a handful of dust, a drop of water, flame, and finally the speech of all living creatures.

On completion of the full revelation of Deep Knowledge, the Faery king said, *"O King of the Elements for sure you know much; but now I have made you to know the secret things of the green Earth that is Mother of you and of Mary too."* The revelation of the Deep Knowledge of the Realm of Faery was finished. Christ knew even more now than he had brought with him from Heaven into human incarnation. His knowledge of Heaven, Earth and the Realm of Faery was now complete. Note that he accepted all of this information, all of the runes, all of the various non-human speech, without thought, question or comment. However the final comment by the Faery king *"the green Earth that is Mother of you and of Mary too"* did cause Christ to stop and think. This was the only mystery that he pondered over. All of the other wonderful and mysterious things told to him by the Faery king he accepted without thought or question but now that the identity of his true mother, the green Earth, was revealed he stopped to think about this important Mystery. Note that the Faery king points out that the green Earth is mother to Mary as well as to Jesus, i.e. to humans as well as to Christ. This is important, and emphasizes in the strongest way possible that the Deep Knowledge of the realm of Faery also consists of developing a loving, caring relationship with the green Earth who is mother to Christ, humans and Faeries alike. It is our common meeting place and the one great link that holds us all together, and will reveal more to us than even the Faery king could do with his revelations of the Deep Knowledge.

We know from the Bible and other texts that Christ took the knowledge he had brought with him and the Deep Knowledge learned from the Faery king and gave it out freely to all who would listen, until he was silenced on the cross. Interestingly the Faery legend does not stop with the passing of the information by the Faery king but goes on to tell what happened to both him and Jesus. First we are told that once the Faery king left the infant Christ in Bethlehem, *"he got to his people [and] they put him alive into a hollow of the earth and covered him up, because of his shining eyes, and the green youth that was about him as a garland. And when Christ was nailed upon the Cross, Deep Knowledge went back into the green world, and passed into the grass and the sap in trees, and the flowing wind, and the dust that swirls and is gone."*

When he returned to the Realm of Faery his people saw that he was no longer the old, blind desert king but was once again the embodiment of the Green Life, the sap that runs in the trees, the waters that sparkle in the streams, the winds that freshen the air, and they joyfully returned him to his rightful place deep in the earth. His life had come full circle from the sorrow of sorrows at recognizing the Queen of Heaven to the joy of being the life-force behind the Deep Knowledge. The final sentence of this short myth is not to be found in the Bible but tells us where we too can find the Deep Knowledge and makes it clear that it is available to all, always.

Several times throughout her life Fiona recognised other Faeries like her that were living amongst the human race and she seems to have been able to recognise humans who still carry the mixed blood of Faruane and Mo-an in their veins. As discussed earlier, her friend and confidant Catherine Janvier seems to have been one such mixed blood acquaintance and also, perhaps, Edith Wingate Rinder. After concluding the above tale of the Deep Knowledge, Fiona went on to address Catherine Janvier and said:

> *"All this is of the wisdom of the long ago, and you and I are those who know how ancient it is, how remoter far than when Mary, at the bidding of her little son, threw up into the firmament the tears of an old man.*
> *It is old, old —*
>
> *'Thousands of years, thousands*
> *of years,*
> *If all were told.'*
>
> *Is it wholly unwise, wholly the fantasy of a dreamer to insist, in this late day, when the dust of ages and the mists of the present hide from us the Beauty of the World, that we can regain our birthright only by leaving our cloud-palaces of the brain, and becoming one with the cosmic life of which, merely as men, we are no more than a perpetual phosphorescence?"*

Here she specifically links Catherine Janvier to Faery by saying *"you and I are those who know how ancient it is"*. Often in her dedications, letters and other personal comments Fiona revealed much more than she did in the text of her stories, poems, runes and plays. It was in these personal asides to friends that she spoke most openly and freely as a Faery.

As well as giving out these important pieces of Faery mythology Fiona also wrote of how the Faeries feel about humankind so dominating the planet that originally we both shared as equal custodians. Her poem *The Crimson Moon* expresses the Faery belief that one day they shall again walk the surface of the earth as we do.

> *Behind the Legions of the Sun, the Star Battalions of the night,*
> *The reddening of the West I see, from morn till dusk, from dusk till light.*
> *A day must surely come at least, and that day soon,*
> *When the Hidden People shall march out beneath the Crimson Moon.*
>
> *Our palaces shall crumble then, our towers shall fall away,*
> *And on the plains our burning towns shall flaunt a desolate day:*

The cities of our pride shall wear tiaras of red flame,
And all our phantom glory be a wind-blown name.

What shall our vaunt be on that day, or who thereon shall hear
The laughter of our laughing lips become the wail of fear?
Our vaunt shall be the windy dust in eddies, far and wide,
The hearing, theirs who follow us with swift and dreadful stride.

A cry of lamentation, then, shall sweep from land to land:
A myriad waving hands shall shake above a myriad strand:
The Day shall swoon before a Shade of vast ancestral Night,
Till a more dreadful Morn awake to flood and spume of light.

This is the prophecy of old, before the roaming tribes of Man
Spread Multitude athwart the heirdom of an earlier Clan —
Before the gods drank Silence, and hid their way with cloud,
And Man uprose and claimed the Earth and all the starry crowd.

So Man conceived and made his dream, till at last he smiled to see
Its radiant skirts brush back the stars from Immortality:
He crowned himself with the Infinite, and gave his Soul a Home,
And then the quiet gods awoke and blew his life to foam.

This is the Dream I see anew, when all the West is red with light,
Behind the Legions of the Sun, the Star Battalions of the night.
Verily the day may come at last, and that day soon,
When the Hidden people shall march out beneath the Crimson Moon.

As mentioned elsewhere in this book, this theme is stated quite specifically in the short story *Cuilidh Mhoire* where Fiona says, "*And what the people were then, in the many, they still are in the few; though now for the most part only where the Great Disenchantment has not yet wholly usurped the fading dominion of the Great Enchantment.*" Being pushed aside by the uncaring masses of humankind is obviously of concern to the Faeries and it should be just as much of concern to humans.

There are not too many examples of human mythology and Faery mythology meeting or overlapping but the joining of myths happens from time to time when we speak of the many physical places in our world that we consider sacred or special. Some of these locations are likewise considered sacred or special by the Faeries. For example, the Faeries consider Avalon a real and special place, just as our own mythology tells us, and it is one of the few places where the two worlds are very close. There is much pointless debate as to exactly where the 'real' Avalon, or the 'true' Avalon, can be found in this world. Some say Glastonbury in England, some say the Isle of Arran in Scotland, others say this place or that place. It does not matter. It is true that these and other physical locations in our world are places of special power and importance, but the real Avalon, the true Avalon, is found in the heart. One point of agreement between the human understanding and the Faery understanding of Avalon is that its name connects it with apple trees. The Faery verse Fiona gave us that deals with Avalon is:

Song of Apple-Trees

Song of Apple-trees, honeysweet and murmurous,
Where the swallows flash and shimmer as
They thrid the foamwhite maze,
Breaths of far-off Avalon are blown to us,
Come down to us,
Avalon of the Heart's Desire, Avalon of the Hidden Ways!

Song of Apple-blossom, when the myriad leaves are gleaming
Like undersides of small green waves in foam of shallow seas,
One may dream of Avalon, lie dreaming,
Dreaming, dreaming,
Till wandering through dim vales of dusk the stars hang in the trees.

Song of Apple-trees, honeysweet and murmurous,
When the night-wind fills the branches with a sound of muffled oars,
Breaths of far-off Avalon are blown to us,
Come down to us,
Avalon of the Heart's Desire, Avalon of the Hidden Shores.

Avalon has become firmly connected with the Arthurian mythology, and Merlin, the archetypical magician from that mythology, is shared by human and Faery alike. It should be pointed out that our legends of him say that he is of Faery, and so to be accurate this is a case where humankind has borrowed from Faery mythology and usurped this famous Faery magician for our own symbolic use. Fiona wrote the following interesting poem concerning Merlin and one of his creations.

The Last Fay

I have wandered where the cuckoo fills
The woodlands with her magic voice:
I have wandered on the brows of hills
Where the last heavenward larks rejoice:
Far I have wandered by the wave,
By shadowy loch and swaying stream,
But never have I found the grave
of him who made me a wandering Dream.
If I could find that lonely place
And him who lies asleep therein,
I'd bow my head and kiss his face
And sleep and rest and peace would win.

He made me, he who lies asleep
Hidden in some forgotten spot
Where winds sweep and rains weep
And foot of wayfarer cometh not:
He made me, Merlin, ages ago,
He shaped me in an idle hour,
He made a heart of fire to glow
And hid it in an April shower!
For I am but a shower that calls
A thin sweet song of rain, and pass:
Even the wind-whirled leaf that falls
Lingers awhile within the grass,
But I am blown from hill to vale,
From vale to hill like a bird's cry
That shepherds hear a far-off wail
And woodfolk as a drowsy sigh.

And I am tired, whom Merlin made.
I would lie down in the heart of June
And fall asleep in a leafy shade
And wake till in the Faery Moon

Merlin shall rise our lord and king,
To leave for aye the tribes of Man,
And let the clarion summons ring
The kingdom of the Immortal Clan.
If but in some green place I'd see
An ancient tangled moss-like beard
And half-buried boulder of a knee
I should not flutter away afeared!
With leap of joy, with low glad cry
I'd sink beside the Sleeper fair:
He would not grudge my fading sigh
In the ancient stillness brooding there.

The human-based mythology of King Arthur contains many stories of him and his knights setting off on deer hunts. Invariably not long after the chase is under way something of a magical nature happens to one or all of the hunters. The deer, or reindeer, is one of the animals to look out for in these myths and legends, as it is an indicator of the presence of Faeries or the closeness of an entryway into the Realm of Faery. The great collection of Gaelic lore *Carmina Gadelica* has many runes warning of the dangers of contact with the Faeries but in a footnote on page 375 there is a short lullaby, said to have come from the Faeries themselves, called *Bainne nam fiadh* (milk of the deer/reindeer) that says,

> *On milk of reindeer I was raised,*
> *On milk of reindeer was nurtured,*
> *On milk of reindeer beneath the ridge of storms,*
> *On crest of hill and mountain.*

This is just one example of a little symbolic connection that could easily be missed. When deer, or reindeer, appear in folk tales, songs and legends it means that the following part of the story is set in the Realm of Faery.

Another little creature that is important in the mythology of Faery is the bee, specifically the wild bee. It is easy to miss or ignore Fiona's frequent references to bees that are scattered throughout her work, as they often seem to be mentioned only in passing. The very fact that she did mention them so often though should alert us to the fact that they are important. In an earlier chapter I quoted from Fiona's short story

The Anointed Man from her collection called *Under the Dark Star*. This is the tale of the Faeries giving Alasdair Achanna the Faery sight. The quotation says, *"But the place is far, and the hour is hidden. No man may seek that for which there can be no quest. Only the wild bees know of it, but I think they must be the bees of Magh-Mell. And there no man that liveth may wayfare — yet."* In the earlier chapter I was focusing on her use of the word 'yet', but here I want to pay attention to the reference to wild bees. As said earlier, the name Magh-Mell is another name for the Realm of Faery. So these knowledgeable little bees are ones that have come from the land of the Great Enchantment and they have the knowledge of where to find it. This is a common motif in Fiona's stories when bees crop up — they are wise, and we can learn from their knowledge many things that are hidden.

One of the longest discussions on these little winged honey-makers is in the tale *The Lords of Wisdom*, which can be found in her collection called *The Winged Destiny*. The opening paragraphs form a discussion on the secret lore of bees and then, abruptly, the tale switches to a short vignette of the young Christ learning even more Deep Knowledge from the bees; and this time, his mother Mary shares the experience. Thomas B. Mosher reprinted this latter part for the American market, but he omitted the opening discussion on the mythology of bees. Here it is (with some irrelevant side-discussions on Gaelic sayings omitted).

"A friend writes to me asking what is 'the wisdom of the wild bees'? He read the phrase, he says, in something I wrote once, and also in an Oban paper last year, quoted there as a Hebridean saying. I am not sure if I heard it in English. But in Gaelic, either as 'the old wisdom of the bees,' or 'the secret knowledge of the bees,' the phrase occurs in tales of the islanders of Tiree, Coll, Iona, Colonsay, and Islay... In Iona, some years ago, I heard an old woman speak of the robin-redbreast as 'St. Columba's Companion,' and of the wild bees as his children: 'They have Colum's wisdom,' she said. But I imagine in most cases the phrase is used without much thought of the lost or time-worn meaning, as are the other phrases I have given. 'Ask the wild bee for what the Druids knew,' and 'ask the children of the heather where Fionn sleeps,' and the like, point to an old association of the wild bee and ancient wisdom. And, doubtless, the story teller of today might naturally use figuratively or directly allude to a creature so familiar to him: as, last year, in one of the isles, a shepherd speaking to me ended his narrative with 'and I would go to that country, and look till I found, if I had the three wisdoms of the bee, that can find its way in the grass, and over

the widest water, and across the height of hills.' Here, of course, is meant the natural knowledge of the bee... and not long ago I heard a phrase used by a Gaelic preacher... 'Who was it put wisdom on the bee, teaching her the direction of the fields of the air, and the homeway to the hive on hillside or in glen; or who showed the salmon to leave the depths of the sea, and come up narrow streams; or who gave the raven the old wisdom of the hills?' In Ross, I was told by a man of the Gairloch, they speak... of the little bees as 'lords of wisdom' or 'the little kings of wisdom.' It is a fine phrase, that... the lords of wisdom: and not one to forget."

All of this is making abundantly clear the importance of bees in Faery mythology and the fact that they have knowledge of many things we do not. The last little phrase in the above quotation is not so much a comment but a direct instruction – 'do not forget this, it is important.'

The second part of this little tale of bees is in a sense a continuation of the other important Christ story related above, *How Deep Knowledge Came to the Child Jesus.* It carries on the theme of the Christ learning much Deep Knowledge from the Green World and imparting it to Mary. Once again it is a very peculiar mix of Christian belief and ancient Faery mythology.

"One day when the young Christ was nine years old he saw Mary walking by a thicket. He ran and hid in the thicket, and sent three wishes of love to her, and gave to each the beat of two wings and the pulse of song. The first rose on wings of blue and sank into the sky, carrying a prayer of Mary. The second rose on white wings and fled seawards by the hills of the west, carrying a hope of Mary. The third rose on wings of green, and sank to the grasses, carrying a dream of Mary. Then a voice came from the thicket; a voice so sweet as to send the birds to the branches ...

The Yellow Star, O Mary, to the bird of the blue wing! ...

The rainbow, O Mary, to the white bird! ...

The wild bee, O Mary, to the green bird! ...

At that, Mary worshipped. 'O God in the thicket,' she said, 'sweet the songs and great the beauty. But lo! The birds are gone.' Then Christ came out of the thicket, and took her hand. 'Mother,' said the child, 'no trouble to your heart, dear, because of the Yellow Star. Your prayer was that my Father would not forget His secret promise. The sun is steadfast, and so I say that the Yellow Star is set upon your prayer. And no trouble to your heart, Mother, because of the Rainbow to the white bird: for your hope was for the gates of the west and the hidden garden of Peace: and even now the gates are open, and spices and balms are on the green wave that flows the long way east of the sun and west of the moon. But as to the wild bee, Mother, of that I cannot speak.'

At that, Mary was sad, for she knew when a Druid of the east had told her to give her son the friendship of the wind, of the blown dust, of the grass, of the leaf, and of the wild bee, she had done all these things but the last. So she stood and wept.

Then the young Christ, her son, called to a bee that was among the foam-white pastures.

'What was your dream, Mother?' he said.

'My dream,' said Mary, 'was that I should know death at the last, for in the flesh I am a woman, and that of me that is mortal desireth death.'

So Christ asked the wild bee. But the bee said, 'Can you see the nine hundred and ninety-nine secret roads of the air?'

'No,' said the child.

'It is on one of these roads,' said the wild bee, 'that Mary's dream went.'

So when Mary, sad at heart, but in this thing only, went back to the house where she dwelt and made ready the supper for that day's end, Christ gave friendship to the wild bee, and became a bee, and floated above the pastures. And when he came home at twilight he knew all the secrets of the little people of the air.

That night, after the meal was done, he stood looking at Mary and Joseph.

'I have known many wisdoms,' he said, 'but no wisdom like the wisdom of the wild bee. But I have whispered to them a secret thing, and through the years and the ages they will not forget. And some of the children of men shall hear the wild bees, and many shall call upon them; and to that little clan of the unwise and foolish, as they shall ever be accounted, I will send the bees of wisdom and of truth.'

And Joseph said, 'Are the bees then so wise?'

But Mary whispered; 'I do not think it is of the wild bees of the pastures that the Christ my son speaks, but of the wild bees of the Spirit.'

Christ slept, and put his hand in Mary's, and she had no fear: and that of her which was of heaven deepened in joy, and that of her which was mortal had peace. But Joseph lay awake, and wondered why to a little clan of those held foolish and unwise should come, as secret wings in the dark, the sound and breath of an ancient wisdom."

There is much intense and deep symbolism contained in this short piece, the full unravelling of which I must leave for another book. But take note of the passage, "*Christ gave friendship to the wild bee, and became a bee, and... when he came home at twilight he knew all the secrets of the little people of the air... 'I have known many wisdoms... but no wisdom like the wisdom of the wild bee. But I have whispered to them a secret thing, and through the years and the ages they will not forget...' And Joseph said, 'Are the bees then so wise?' But Mary whispered; 'I do not think it is of the wild bees of the pastures that the Christ my son speaks, but of the wild bees of the Spirit.'"* This is another example of Christ learning much previously unknown lore from the Faeries and the creatures of the Green World, but notice this time he reciprocated by giving the wild bees in return *"a secret thing."* This tells us that not only will the wild bees of the Spirit be able to tell us much of the Realm of Faery that we may not know, but they too can tell us secret things of the Christ that have not (so far) been revealed in his teachings to humankind.

Chapter Eight

⨳AERY ⸙UNES

The first four winds are the 'Gaoth tuath' (the North Wind), 'Gaoth 'n ear' (the East Wind), 'Gaoth deas' (the South Wind), and 'Gaoth 'n iar' (the West Wind). The three others are the Breaths of the Grave, of the Depths of the Sea (or Oblivion), and of the Future.

T HE GREAT STOREHOUSE of Gaelic lore collected by Alexander Carmichael in the 19th century as *Carmina Gadelica* contains many runes, sayings and incantations that seem to cover everything imaginable from the daily life of the Gaelic Highlanders and Islanders. The recitation of these runes was an important aspect of daily life for the Gaelic people in ensuring the successful negotiation of their daily business and for the maintenance of their physical and spiritual health. Fiona too gives out many runes in her stories and poems and although these follow much the same patterns of composition as the ones from Carmichael's volumes their intended purposes are quite another thing altogether. Whereas Carmichael's Gaelic runes are easily classifiable into various subjects simply by reading what they say, Fiona's Faery runes are much more abstract and obscure, and therefore more difficult to classify. They are dealing with matters other than those of the world in which we live and work.

The disclosure of these Faery runes was clearly important to Fiona as she started to reveal them right from her first two books, *Pharais* and *The Mountain Lovers*, and continued to do so throughout the rest of her work. It should be pointed out here that when *Pharais* was published, Alexander Carmichael accused William Sharp of having stolen several runes from the manuscript of *Carmina Gadelica*, which he had given on loan to William Sharp, and of having passed these on to Fiona Macleod to use in her book. Carmichael did not know that William and Fiona were one and the same person. While there are several runes in these first two books that do bear a strong resemblance to the ones found in Carmichael's work, there are others that are of a similar style and layout but which deal with subjects not to be found in *Carmina Gadelica*. For example, in *The Mountain Lovers*, Fiona gives the *Rann-an-h'Aoise*, or, as it is in English, the *Cry to Age*. It says,

> *O thou that on the hills and wastes of Night art Shepherd,*
> *Whose folds are flameless moons and icy planets,*
> *Whose darkling way is gloomed with ancient sorrows:*
> *Whose breath lies white as snow upon the olden,*
> *Whose sigh it is that furrows breast grown milk-less,*
> *Whose weariness is in the loins of man*
> *And is the barren stillness of the woman:*
> *O thou whom all would 'scape and all must meet,*
> *Thou that the Shadow art of Youth-Eternal,*
> *The gloom that is the hush'd air of the Grave,*
> *The sigh that is between last parted love,*
> *The light for aye withdrawn from weary eyes,*
> *The tide from stricken hearts forever ebbing!*
> *O thou, the Elder Brother whom none loveth,*
> *Whom all men hail with reverence and mocking,*
> *Who broodeth on the peaks of herbless summits,*
> *Yet dreamest in the eyes of babes and children:*
> *Thou, Shadow of the Heart, the Brain, the Life,*
> *Who art that dusk, What is, that is, already Has been,*
> *To thee this rune of the-fathers-to-the-sons,*
> *And of the sons to the sons, and mothers to new mothers —*
> *To thee who art Aois,*
> *To thee who art Age!*
>
> *Breathe thy frosty breath upon my hair, for I am weary;*
> *Lay thy frozen hand upon my bones that they support not,*
> *Put thy chill upon the blood that it sustain not,*
> *Place the crown of thy fulfilling on my forehead,*
> *Throw the silence of thy spirit on my spirit,*
> *Lay the balm and benediction of thy mercy*
> *On the brain-throb and the heart-pulse and the life-spring —*

For thy child that bows his head is weary,
For thy child that bows his head is weary.
I the shadow am that seeks the Darkness.
Age, that hath the face of Night unstarr'd and moonless,
Age that doth extinguish star and planet,
Moon and sun and all the fiery worlds,
Give me now thy darkness and thy silence!

In *The Mountain Lovers* this particular rune is spoken by an old blind man who believes he is about to die; indeed he seeks death. On a first reading this is the theme that comes out quite clearly, but reading a little deeper, and understanding some of the more obscure references that Fiona often used, a different meaning starts to reveal itself. The *Elder Brother* in line 14 and the *Shadow* in line 18 are references to the dark Faery god Dalua (see Chapter Six) who does not appear in traditional Gaelic or Celtic lore, mythology or runes at all. This shows that the old man is praying to a specific god of death, the Faery god Dalua, rather than just the faceless, nameless 'death' that otherwise appears opaquely in the rune. This particular, rather dark and brooding rune could not have come from *Carmina Gadelica,* where there are no prayers to death under any name. It came instead directly from Fiona's own native Faery lore.

A whole collection of these non-Gaelic runes can be found in an early article Fiona wrote in December 1895 for *Harper's Magazine* entitled *From the Hebrid Isles.* Part of this long essay says,

"*The first four winds are the 'Gaoth tuath' (the North Wind), 'Gaoth 'n ear' (the East Wind), 'Gaoth deas' (the South Wind), and 'Gaoth 'n iar' (the West Wind). The three others are the Breaths of the Grave, of the Depths of the Sea (or Oblivion), and of the Future. In the first couplet the North Wind is alluded to as the breath of the pole-star. A more literal rendering of the original of the second would be,*

'By the wild strained voice on the summits,
When the feet of the dead folk are knowing
The sound of its flowing.'

This is an allusion to the ancient Celtic custom of burying the dead with their feet to the east. It is believed that the Wind of the Resurrection will come from the east, and so the righteous dead will be awakened by its breath across the world.

From this has come the tradition that the dead know whenever the east wind blows, and that in this way tidings reach them of the two worlds, that which they have left and that beyond the grave, or 'the sleep.' In the Outer Hebrides it is commonly believed that those about to die soon can feel 'the breath on the soles of the feet.' In the third couplet a little more expansion would again be more explicit, e.g.:

'By the high blithe cry on the rivers,
On the straths and the glens and the Machar,
Where the Heat-star moveth,'

The machar is any flat (generally a sandy, or at any rate sea-margining, plain), and the Heat-star is supposed to be the source of the moist south or southwest wind. The West Wind, again, blows from the Land of Rainbows, a poetic isles-idiom for the seaward west.

I.

By the Voice in the corries,
When the Pole-star breatheth:

By the Voice on the summits
The dead feet know:

By the soft wet cry
When the Heat-star troubleth:

By the plaining and moaning
Of the Sigh of the Rainbows:

By the four white winds of the world,
Whose father the golden Sun is,

Whose mother the wheeling Moon is,
The North and the South and the East and the West:

By the four good winds of the world,
That Man knoweth,
That One dreadeth,
That God blesseth —

Be all well
On mountain and moorland and lea,
On loch-face and lochan and river,
On shore and shallow and sea!

II.

By the Voice of the Hollow
Where the worm dwelleth:

By the Voice of the Hollow
Where the sea-wave stirs not:

By the Voice of the Hollow
That Sun hath not seen yet:
By the three dark winds of the world;
The chill dull breath of the Grave,
The breath from the depths of the Sea,
The breath of To-morrow:

By the white and dark winds of the world,
The four and the three that are seven,
That Man knoweth,
That One dreadeth,
That God blesseth —

Be all well
On mountain and moorland and lea,
On loch-face and lochan and river,
On shore and shallow and sea!

Were this an old rune the tenth line would probably have run, 'Whose <u>mother</u> the golden Sun is,' for with the ancient Celts the sun was feminine. I do not know, but surmise that the line 'That One dreadeth' is an allusion to an old Celtic saying that at the last day the Evil One will be scourged out of the world

'By the white and dark winds....
The four and the three that are seven.'"

131

There is an enormous amount of information given out in this short passage but, in the bigger picture, it is important to note that this rune is basically about seven different winds – four for each direction and three for the Grave, the Sea and the Future. Nowhere in the traditional Gaelic lore is there to be found a rune dealing with seven winds and nowhere are there any runes dealing with colours and the winds in combination. These are fairly and squarely Faery matters.

But this theme of coloured winds and of these winds being connected with life, death, joy and sorrow, crops up time and time again in Fiona's writings. See Chapter Eleven for a full discussion of one of Fiona's more important runes, the *Invocation of Peace,* which makes extensive use of colours and winds. There is something of great worth here that she wished us to learn. William Sharp once related that his old Hebridean nurse Barbara gave him a rune that uses the four directions of space in a very similar manner to the opening lines of the above article:

The Four Stars of Destiny

Reul Near (Star of the East), Give us kindly birth;
Reul Deas (Star of the South), Give us great love;
Reul Siar (Star of the West), Give us great age;
Reul Tuath (Star of the North), Give us Death.

Note that before Fiona gives the actual text of the rune in her article above she first of all explains some of the more obscure meanings it contains. Much of this explanation is taken up with death. Death is also mentioned in the last line of nurse Barbara's rune. If you read Fiona's writings in chronological order, both her published books and her magazine articles, you will note that death is an important central theme and that many of the sub-plots or explanatory passages deal with various aspects of death and dying. Considering that her mission, as it were, was to reveal the secrets of the Faery tradition to humankind through her writings then the fact that she chose the subject of physical death as her first topic for discussion shows how important this is to the Faeries and, therefore, to anyone interested in understanding the Faery mysteries. It proved, however, to be a bit intimidating, too direct and blunt for the average Victorian reader to deal with, and her later output softened considerably and she hardly touched on the subject of death again. This whole article from *Harper's Magazine* is a good example of how

Fiona, in her early days, had not yet learned to put Faery lore into words, images and symbols that we humans, ignorant of such things, could understand. As they stand at the moment they take a lot of reading and re-reading, a lot of thought, meditation and dissection, before the wealth of information contained therein starts to become clear. But with a certain amount of effort the rewards are high.

Later in this same *Hebrid Isles* article she gives a rune called *The Rune of the Reading of the Spirit*, which says:

By that which dwells within thee,	*(the soul)*
By the lamps that shine upon me,	*(the eyes)*
By the white light I see litten	
From the brain now sleeping stilly,	*(the light on the brow)*
By the silence in the hollows,	*(the ears)*
By the wind that slow subsideth,	*(the slacking breath)*
By the life-tide slowly ebbing,	
By the death-tide slowly rising,	*(the pulsing blood)*
By the slowly waning warmth,	
By the chill that slowly groweth,	
By the dusk that slowly creepeth,	
By the darkness near thee,	
By the darkness round thee,	*(swoon, or trance)*
By the darkness o'er thee —	
O'er thee, round thee, on thee —	
By the one that standeth	
At thy side and waiteth	*(the soul)*
Dumb and deaf and blindly,	
By the one that moveth,	
Bendeth, riseth, watcheth,	*(the phantom)*
By the dim Grave-Spell upon thee,	
By the Silence thou has wedded...	
May the way thy feet are treading,	
May the tangled lines now crooked,	
Clear as moonlight lie before me!	

Here again death is staring us in the face. This particular rune could fit into the genre of books from other religions and philosophies that have come to be known as Books of the Dead – for example *The Egyptian Book of the Dead* or *The Tibetan Book of the Dead* – which are basically manuals intended to prepare the spirit for what to expect in the life after physical death. Notice that this rune is not solely in the First Person. Line 1 refers to '*thee*' and line 2 and the final line refer to '*me.*' The unidentified narrator is witnessing, or perhaps even aiding, some other person to make the transition from this life to the afterlife. The final three lines imply that this witness is there to guide the released human spirit along a path that leads away from the physical world and deep into the Realm of Faery.

A final rune from this important *Hebrid Isles* article is a 'closing' rune used to thank and send away any Faery contact you have been working with once your need for contact has stopped. It is far removed from the 'banishing' rituals and spells to be found in medieval grimoires and magical tomes that banish summoned demons back to Hades. The wording of those spells is often threatening and damning but this one is actually laying a complex blessing of thanks upon the departing Faery, a very different state of affairs altogether. Fiona says in her article that it is originally from the Shetland Isles and in her article she gives it first in the peculiar Shetland Norn dialect but, later, gives what she calls the Celtic version (for which read 'Faery') with explanations.

It is interesting that she makes this emphasis on Shetland. The Shetland archipelago lies in the extreme north of the British Isles, not too far from the Faroe Islands and, from there, north to Iceland. In Chapter Four I discuss another piece of Fiona's writings that specifically talks of the Faeries having removed to the far north, away from the Scottish Hebrides and Highlands, and the fact that there is a different order of Faeries in Iceland. Here she is again pointing out the importance of looking to the far north and the fact that there are different orders or types of Faeries, perhaps even ones unique to Shetland. The 'Celtic' version of this rune, with explanations, says,

By the twelve white apostles,
By the eleven evangelists,
And by the ten holy commandments,
By the Nine Angels,
By the Flowing of the Eight Rivers,
By the seven stars of the World,
By the six Days of Creation,
By the Five who pass at death,
By the four Gospels,

Faery Runes

By the three who weave and sever,
By the two white Beings clad in green,
And by the Lonely Spirit (Spioraid aonarach) —
    To the mountain hollow!
    To the hill hollow!
    To the hollow i' the hill!

The allusions in the first, second, third and seventh lines, to the Pleiades in the sixth line, and to the Fates in the tenth line are plain enough.

'The Five who pass at Death' is, I take it, an allusion to a very ancient, obscure and rare Celtic legend: that an hour before dawn, on the day we die, five shadowy beings come out of the darkness, look at us, beckon and vanish. These are the Shadows of those of our race who have crossed the frontier of death: the Shadow of our own soul; the Shadow of the grave; the Shadow of what shall be; and the Shadow of the Unmentionable and the Unknown.

I am not sure what the eleventh line means. Possibly the two white beings are the Soul and the Body. Possibly the allusion is to the twin brothers Life and Death. The mention of the colour-epithet 'green' is congruous, for green is at once the sacred, the mystic and the demoniac colour. The 'guid-folk' of the hills are clad in green; the 'Bandruidh' or 'Cailleach,' that fatal siren of the hillside, is always seen in a green robe; 'Black Donald' himself, when he appears to mortal vision, is always a 'tall, gaunt stranger clad in green'; the road to Paradise that leads out of the Valley of the Shadow of Death is 'an upland way of shining green'; the souls of the blest are visible in raiment a green as pale as the leaves of the lime when the sun shines through them; and the Spirit of God is sometimes revealed as 'a green gloom tremulous with golden light.'

Nor, again, am I sure as to the meaning of the twelfth line. Possibly the allusion is to the Holy Ghost; though the usual Spioraid Naomh could have been used more readily and as impressively as Spioraid Aonanarach, or Aonarach. Aonanarach can mean 'desolate' or 'deserted' as well as 'solitary' or 'lonely'. Probably, therefore, the Spioraid Aonanarach is the Prince of Darkness. The line was also repeated to me with the terminal aonanarach; and so would run, 'The one that goeth in loneliness.' This is obviously translatable variously. Were the allusion to God, probably the line would run, 'And by Himself that is forever alone' (i.e., above and beyond all). Allusively God is almost invariably spoken of as 'E-Fèin', 'Himself.' To some the Gaelic words would have a sombre significance, as though indicative of the Evil Spirit, who, moreover, is supposed to be liege lord of all human seeming though non-human creatures, such as the guid-folk, the wood dwellers, the wave-haunters and the like. It has been suggested to me that 'the one that goeth in loneliness' or 'the one that walketh alone,' is no other than the Wandering Jew ... Judas ... As to the 'nine angels' of the fourth line, I have not been able to ascertain from any one, or from any book, who the nine angels are, why nine in number or what their mission is or was ... Since I wrote this it has occurred to me that possibly the 'Nine Angels' may be the 'nine angelic orders.' Or, again, it may be a half-Pagan, half-Christian confusion with the Nine Muses... It is possible that the allusion to the eight rivers, in the fifth line, is purely Celtic. I remember having heard in my childhood that the Fountain of Living Water in the centre of Paradise is fed by eight great rivers. Four of these flow eternally, respectively, from the east, the south, the west, and the north. Of the other four, two flow into the Fountain of Living Water from below, namely, the river of human tears and the river of human hopes; and two forever descend in rainbow-dews, the river of Peace, that is the benediction of God, and the river of Beauty, that is the 'anail nan speur', the breath of the skies — the loveliness that is pain, 'an acain Pharais', 'the moan of Heaven', and the loveliness that is a chant of joy, 'Seinn Pharais'.

Once again this rune and the succeeding commentary are full of previously unknown symbolism and attributions straight from the Realm of Faery. Note that the elaborate symbolism and powerful images invoked by the twelve opening lines are all just leading up to the last three lines which simply ask the Faery to return to its subterranean home, the hollow hills. The overall style of this rune with a countdown of people and things in ever decreasing size of groups is typical of many of the Gaelic runes found in *Carmina Gadelica* but, as before, the subjects of these particular groups are not typical of the Gaelic at all. In her discussion on this complex rune Fiona implies in several places that she does not fully understand what some of it means. This may indeed be the case but this was also a technique she used frequently to give out as much related lore and connected symbolism as she could in the form of a discussion on the obscure points of the rune. This prevented the information coming across as too much like an instruction book or a formal lesson. I believe she knew intimately the full meanings of all of these Faery runes but found it better to feign uncertainty and use this device as a way of revealing more and more related lore.

Her comment, *"'The Five who pass at Death' is, I take it, an allusion to a very ancient, obscure and rare Celtic legend"* is an example of another device she employed from time to time. Rather than coming straight out and saying such-and-such a thing is from the Realm of Faery she would claim it to be rare, ancient, obscure, or a phrase that has all-but died out from the Gaelic. This assertion, more often than not, is not true. As I have said before, by simply substituting the word Faery for whenever Fiona says 'Gaelic' or 'Celtic', the real meaning becomes clearer. In this case the Five are unknown in Celtic legend or Gaelic folklore. What then follows is another example of what to expect when physical death approaches. *"These are the Shadows of those of our race who have crossed the frontier of death: the Shadow of our own soul; the Shadow of the grave; the Shadow of what shall be; and the Shadow of the Unmentionable and the Unknown."* The Shadows are only shades in this world. In their own realm they become clear, solid and tangible – and unthreatening.

Her long discussion on the colour green and its links to the Faery tradition highlights that this is nothing less than a Faery rune and that the symbolism it contains can only be fully understood when the reader has a sound and full knowledge of Faery lore. By supplying more and more connections with, in this case, the colour green, Fiona is helping to fill the reader's imagination with a great deal of important, relevant and useful imagery and links that can all be put to practical use in future Faery studies and visits to their realm. Note also that in this section she drops her usual pretence of saying this is all old, forgotten Gaelic lore. Instead she uses very clear and positive statements like, "for green *is* at once the sacred, the mystic and the demoniac colour," "The 'guid-folk' of the hills *are* clad in green," " the 'Bandruidh' … *is* always seen in a green robe," " 'Black Donald' himself… *is* always… clad in green," " the road to Paradise… *is* green," " the souls of the blest *are*… green," and "the Spirit of God *is* sometimes revealed as a green gloom tremulous with golden light" (emphasis added). There is no need to wonder here if this is from some source other than Faery or miss the importance she is placing on the symbolism of the colour green.

The lengthy discussion that follows on the identity of the "Lonely Spirit" of line 12 changes the tone quite significantly. Gone are the clear, exact and unarguable connections of the preceding paragraph to be replaced by speculation and, again, inferences that some if not all of this has come from Celtic and/or Gaelic lore. If you lay aside the confusing details of different Gaelic words and differing interpretations as to their true meaning, what she is really pointing out is that in the Faery tradition the Holy Spirit, God and Dalua are all so closely connected that they are inseparable. Although she has not used the specific name Dalua in her discussion it is clear that this is who she is referring to by her use of the title "Prince of Darkness" and, especially, her emphasis on loneliness and desolation, all names and attributions given to Dalua throughout Faery lore. This is repeated by her comment on the *"liege lord of all human seeming though non-human creatures, such as the guid-folk, the wood dwellers, the wave-haunters and the like"* which is also another description of Dalua. The description 'human seeming though non-human creatures' reminds us of the story of Faruane in Chapter Seven where we are told that the Faery Faruane and the human Mo-an produced offspring that looked human in appearance but were Faery in essence.

In the final section on the Eight Rivers she returns to her device of being vague when she says, *"I remember having heard in my childhood..."*, a claim that is impossible to verify, and a claim that implies a Gaelic source for what follows as Fiona was supposed to have been born and raised in the Gaelic-speaking Hebrides of Scotland. But the detailed picture she paints of four rivers flowing eternally from the four directions, and two rivers flowing in and two flowing out of Paradise, is not Celtic or Gaelic but is from Faery.

The wealth of valuable lore and detailed symbolism contained in this one short Faery rune is astonishing, and far outweighs anything to be found in the human Gaelic lore as recorded by Alexander Carmichael in his nonetheless very valuable *Carmina Gadelica*. I commented above that Carmichael accused Fiona Macleod of plagiarism in her earlier works by not acknowledging the access she had had to his manuscript, but in a later piece called *The Gael and his Heritage* Fiona makes a comment on a rune from *Carmina Gadelica* that says,

> *Thine is the skill of the Faery Woman,*
> *Thine is the virtue of Bride the calm,*
> *Thine is the faith of Mary the mild,*
> *Thine is the tact of the woman of Greece,*
> *Thine is the beauty of Emer the lovely,*
> *Thine is the tenderness of Darthula delightful,*
> *Thine is the courage of Maebh the strong,*
> *Thine is the charm of Honey-Mouth.*

> *How typically Gaelic this is, with its mixture of Christian and old Celtic and pagan lore, the Virgin Mary and St. Bride, 'Muime Chriosd' (Christ's Foster Mother) alternating with the Fairy Woman and with some dim legend of Helen of Troy, and she again with the fair wife of Cuchulain, the great champion of*

Gaeldom, and with Deirdre (Darthula — Deardhuil — Dearshul as in this Gaelic text), the Helen of the Gael, and with Maeve, the Dark Queen whose name and personality loom so vast and terrible in ancient Gaelic history, and 'Honey-Mouth' (Binne-bheul), whom I take to be Angus, the God of Love.

The *content* of this short rune is not so important, but what is important, as Fiona discusses, is its easy and seamless mixing of Christian, Celtic and Faery lore. This same mixture of traditions runs through all of the runes discussed above. This, if nothing else, should tell us to look to all three of these sources if we wish to fully understand any one of them.

Finally, here is a rune written by Fiona that can be found in the volume *Poems and Dramas.* I give it without comment or analysis. Sometimes it is enough to appreciate just the beauty of these Faery sentiments.

Nine Desires

The desire of the fairy women, dew:
The desire of the fairy host, wind:
The desire of the raven, blood:
The desire of the snipe, the wilderness:
The desire of the seamew, the lawns of the sea:
The desire of the poet, the soft low music of the Tribe of the Green Mantles:
The desire of man, the love of woman:
The desire of women, the little clan:
The desire of the soul, wisdom.

Chapter Nine

THE FOUR CITIES

They had four cities at the four ends of the green diamond that is the world. That in the north was made of earth; that in the east, of air; that in the south, of fire; that in the west, of water.

I N SEVERAL PLACES throughout her writings Fiona speaks of four cities to be found in the Realm of Faery. These are Finias, Falias, Murias and Gorias. These same cities, with variant spellings, appear in several important ancient Gaelic Celtic legends, in particular *The Battle of Moytura* and *The Book of the Invasions of Ireland*. The relevant passage from *The Battle of Moytura* tells us:

"The Tuatha De Danann were in the Northern Islands of the world, studying occult lore and sorcery, druidic arts, witchcraft and magical skills, until they surpassed the sages of the pagan arts. They studied occult lore, secret knowledge and diabolical arts in four cities: Falias, Murias, Gorias and Findias. From Falias was brought the Stone of Fal, which was located in Tara. It used to cry out beneath every king that would take Ireland. From Gorias was brought the Spear which Lug had. No battle was ever sustained against it, or against the man who held it in his hand. From Findias was brought the Sword of Nuada. No one ever escaped from it once it was drawn from its deadly sheath, and no one could resist it. From Murias was brought the Dagda's Cauldron. No company ever went away from it unsatisfied. There were four wizards in those four cities. Morfesa was in Falias; Esras was in Gorias; Uiscias was in Findias; and Semias was in Murias. They were the four poets from whom the Tuatha De learned occult lore and secret knowledge."

There is some debate as to the exact meaning of the name *Tuatha De Danann* but it is usually given as *The People of the Goddess Danu*. However, the more important concern for us at the moment is not the people but the places, namely the four cities. The first thing that is obvious from the text above is that they are important centres of learning. The names given to the subjects that were studied and taught there are a bit archaic to our modern minds but this is irrelevant for our present study. All we need to note is that they were extremely important places of learning and training.

As I said above, the names of these cities are to be found in what are two Gaelic Celtic legends, not Faery legends, but there is a small problem here. There are no words in Old Irish (the language in which these legends were first written down) that use the suffix '*-ias*' which is found on all the city names and all the names of the poet-teachers. This may be our first clue that what is being recorded here is a memory of very early human contact with the Faeries. It is possible that the names of these important places and people *have* been recorded accurately, the explanation for the non-standard Gaelic spelling being that they are not Old Irish at all, but are names that originated in the Realm of Faery. But over time and through repeated re-tellings they have been corrupted somewhat from their original spelling and have been mixed with the Gaelic language.

I suggest this because although the suffix '*-ias*' is not from the Gaelic, the prefix of each city's name *is* from the Gaelic. These four Gaelic prefixes can be translated as '*Fal*' – stone; '*Mur*' – the sea; '*Gor*' – fire, and '*Find*' – air. Anyone familiar with Alchemy, the Western Mystery Tradition, Wicca and several other magical traditions, will note the clear connection between the four cities of the Realm of Faery and the Four Elements used in magical working in the human world. Fiona used groups of four frequently in her writings, and other such groups of four are mentioned at various places throughout this book. She mentions these four cities in the excerpt from *The Chronicles of the Sidhe* quoted in Chapter Four and she also wrote one poem dealing with all four cities together, and four other poems dealing with each one individually. They were clearly important to her and were a facet of Faery lore that she needed to make us aware of. It will therefore be beneficial to look closely at what each of these five poems says. The poem that deals with the four cities collectively is as follows.

The Dirge of the Four Cities

Finias and Falias?
Where are they gone?
Does the wave hide Murias —
Does Gorias know the dawn?
Does not the wind wail
In the city of gems?
Do not the prows sail
Over fallen diadems
And the spires of dim gold
And the pale palaces
Of Murias, whose tale was told
Ere the world was old?

Do women cry Alas!...
Beyond Finias?
Does the eagle pass
Seeing but her shadow on the grass
Where once was Falias:
And do her towers rise
Silent and lifeless to the frozen skies?
And do whispers and sighs
Fill the twilights of Finias
With love that has not grown cold
Since the days of old?

Hark to the tolling of bells
And the crying of wind!
The old spells
Time out of mind,
They are crying before me and behind!
I know no more of my pain,
But am as the wandering rain
Or as the wind's shadow on the grass
Beyond Finias of the Dark Rose:
Or, 'mid the pinnacles and still snows
Of the Silence of Falias,
I go: or am as the wave that idly flows

Where the pale weed in songless thickets grows
Over the towers and fallen palaces
Where the Sea-city was,
The city of Murias.

The naming of this poem as a 'dirge' is important. A dirge is a poem or song in memory of someone or something that has died or gone away. It is an expression of loss and sorrow. The imagery displays very clearly that the four cities have been abandoned and have fallen into disrepair. This may well be as a result of the Faeries having left *en masse* when their education in all-things magical was completed. But remember that the quotation from *The Battle of Moytura* above was written a very long time ago and that written version was based on a much older oral version. Since those times things in this world and in the Realm of Faery have changed. As already discussed in Chapter Four, *The Chronicles of the Sidhe* tells us, or at least strongly implies, that the Faeries at some point abandoned our world and returned to the Northern Islands of the world where the four cities are to be found. But let us not confuse the matter any further by going too deeply into that at the moment!

This poem does not reveal much at all about each of the four cities individually. Rather its purpose is to lament the fact that they are abandoned and deprived of their former glory and beauty. From the words of the narrator it is clear that she is saddened by what she has found there and finds no emotional or spiritual comfort in the deserted and broken streets. The comparisons in the verses between the original states of each city and how they appear now shows that the narrator was familiar with each one before they were abandoned. From this we can safely conclude that the narrator must be of the Faeries. Maybe these lines are the personal reveries of Fiona Macleod herself, perhaps they are autobiographical.

The individual poems for each city tell us more and give us more detail to work with. The first we shall look at is:

Finias

In the torch-lit city of Finias that flames on
the brow of the South
The spear that divideth the heart is held in
a brazen mouth —

*Arias the flame-white keeps it, he whose
laughter is heard
Where never a man has wandered, where
never a god has stirred.*

*High kings have sought it, great queens have
sought it, poets have dreamed —
And ever louder and louder the flame-white
laughter of Arias streamed.*

*For kingdoms shaken and queens forsaken
and high hopes starved in their drouth,
These are the forces ablaze on the walls of
Finias that lightens the South.*

*Forbear, O Arias, forbear, forbear — lift not
the dreadful Spear —
I had but dreamed of thee, Finias, Finias …
now I am stricken … now I am here!*

Although the spellings are slightly different between *The Battle of Moytura* Gaelic version and Fiona's Faery version, it is clear that 'Findias' and 'Finias' are the same city. The name of the poet or guardian though is totally different. The Gaelic version has 'Uiscias' and the Faery version has 'Arias.' Note though that they both bear the Faery suffix '-ias.'

The Gaelic version would appear to be misleading. The prefix of the Gaelic name 'Uisc' means 'water' but the city of Finias is the city of air, not water. Then, just to confuse things even more, according to the Faery version the magical weapon that was brought from Finias was the Spear that the Celtic god Lug later inherited. However, the Gaelic version tells us that it was the Sword, not the Spear, which came from Finias. But in this case, the Spear would actually be a more appropriate symbol as the Spear is connected with fire, and note the frequent use of fire imagery throughout the Faery poem.

What is going on here? This confusion and contradiction of names and Magical Weapons between the Gaelic and Faery versions of the four cities occurs in the other three poems as well. If the old Gaelic versions, as given in *The Battle of Moytura* and *The Book of the Invasions of Ireland*, and these much more modern versions as laid down by Fiona

Macleod, have all come from the same source, namely the realm of Faery, why are there apparent discrepancies between them? The answer is that there are no discrepancies because they are *all* correct. It is our limited understanding that is at fault and this consequently causes us to view these variations as discrepancies or outright mistakes. They are not.

To explain: the magical system that Fiona Macleod brought to us from the Realm of Faery operates under a very different basic premise than do the magical systems of the human world. In our world, consistency in symbolism and magical associations between any one thing and any other is of the utmost importance. To glibly chop and change god/goddess names, magical correspondences, the individual attributions of the Four Quarters, etc. within the traditional magical systems of our world does not and cannot work. Everything has to be stable and consistent, unchanging and unbending, in order for each magical ritual to work and in order for a progression of rituals to be possible. But in the very different Realm of Faery there is no consistency in anything. Change, and constant change, is the basic premise for any serious Faery magical working. This is crucial for the would-be Faery magician to recognise and understand. When you enter the Realm of Faery you must leave aside almost everything that you have already learned and think you know. This theme is repeated throughout this book because it underlies everything Fiona Macleod wrote. It is not as difficult as it may at first appear and it can be done.

But to return to the poem; note the several references to seeking and dreaming, plus the references to the laughter of Arias. The seekers and dreamers who long for Finias without fully understanding the true nature of that which they seek are what cause Arias to laugh. Finias cannot be 'found' in the sense we understand that word to mean in our world. It is more a state of being than a physical location. It can be sought after, it can be searched out and it can be found, but not in our world. The dreams that people have of what they will find there and what they will learn are often based on no more than human desire and wish fulfilment. It is watching the confusion and disillusionment of the lost seekers and the feel-good dreamers that causes Arias to laugh, for he alone knows what Finias truly represents. This may seem unnecessarily cruel and mocking. In our world it would be frowned upon to laugh aloud at the confusion and disillusionment of anyone who seeks after truth and knowledge, but in the Realm of Faery this is quite acceptable. The social norms of behaviour and politeness that we expect in our world do not apply in the Realm of Faery. This is another theme that occurs frequently throughout this book and it is an important one for the seeker after Faery to accept and expect.

The last verse of this poem on Finias switches the narrative into the first person, and the speaker, who is also a seeker and dreamer, realises how wrong her dreams were; for now she has achieved Finias her only comment is *"I had but dreamed of thee, Finias, Finias … now I am stricken … now I am here!"* There is quite a sense of panic in those lines, a sense of "Oh! What have I done?" The overall impression we are starting to get from these poems about the four cities of the Realm of Faery seems to be a clear cry of – keep out! Let's see what the next one says.

Falias

In the forest-grown city of Falias lit by the
falling stars
I have seen the ravens flying like banners of
old wars —
I have seen the snow-white ravens amid the
ice-green spires
Seeking the long-lost havens of all old lost
desires.

O winged desire and broken, once nested in
my heart,
Canst thou, there, give a token, that, even now,
thou art?
From bitter war defeated thou too hadst
flight afar,
When all my joy was cheated ere set of
Morning Star.

Call loud; O ancient Moirias, who dwellest in
that place,
Tell me if lost in Falias my old desire hath
grace?
If now a snow-white raven it haunts the silent
spires
For the old impossible haven 'mid the old
auroral fires?

The guardian in the Gaelic version of this poem is given as Morfesa but here the Faery version says Moirias. Considering that all the cities and the other guardian names end with the Faery suffix '*-ias*' it would seem Moirias is the correct name of the guardian. But, just to repeat, don't get too hung up about consistency in these matters: you won't find it. Another obvious inconsistency is the reference to "*snow-white ravens.*" These cannot be the large, jet-black birds that we know in our world so this tells us that the poem is set fairly and squarely in the Realm of Faery where things often appear as the reverse of our world. Also the motif of birds, animals and even people appearing in pure white is common in early Celtic tales and in later common folklore as an indicator they are of Faery origin.

This poem continues the theme of searching for the fulfilment of dreams and desires. Considering these are Faery poems, these dreams and desires, the longings for a return to the four cities, are the dreams and desires of the Faeries themselves. This lets us know that the Faeries too have their own dreams and desires. They do not necessarily lead a long life full of contentment any more than we do. It also implies that, like humans, they are not necessarily always capable of fulfilling their dreams or desires. From a human point of view this is quite comforting. Many Faery researchers hold the unconscious belief that the inhabitants of the Realm of Faery are in some way emotionally superior to we of the human race. This is not the case. It also seems to mean that the warning to 'keep out' as mentioned above is directed not at humans but at the Faeries. So what happens if humans find their way to these abandoned Faery cities? Will we too be told to keep out? Let's read a little more before we attempt to answer this important question.

The reference in the last line to the "*auroral fires*" reminds us again that these four cities are located in the Northern Islands of the world, specifically the Arctic, as confirmed by *The Chronicles of the Sidhe* discussed in Chapter Four.

Now we need to read Fiona's words concerning the next city.

Gorias

In Gorias are gems,
And pale gold,
Shining diadems
Gathered of old
From the long fragrant hair
Of dead beautiful queens.

There the reaper gleans
Vast opals of white air:
The dawn leans
Upon emerald there:
Out of the dust of kings
The sunrise lifts a cloud of
shimmering wings.

In Gorias of the East
My love was born,
Erias dowered with a sword
And the treasures of the Morn —
But now all the red gems
And the pale gold
Are as the trampled diadems
Of the queens of old
In Gorias the pale-gold.

Have I once heard the least,
But the last breath, again?
No: my love is no more fain
Of Gorias of the East.
Erias hath sheathed this sword
Long, long ago ...
Though in Gorias are gems
And pale gold.

Note that once again the name of the guardian in the Gaelic and Faery versions is slightly different – Esras and Erias respectively. As with the previous poem, I would suggest that the Faery version, Erias, is the better one due to the recurrence of the Faery suffix '*-ias.*'

An important point about this poem is the frequent use of the imagery of gold, gems and diadems. This is a common device found in the early Gaelic Celtic legends, such as *The Battle of Moytura*, indicating a Faery origin. Even today in popular folksongs and folklore the Faeries are often referred to as the *Shining Ones*. The use of words indicating sparkling, shining, shimmering like the sheen and lustre of precious stones and metals, lets the reader know the person or object is from the Realm of Faery, not our mundane human world.

The main themes in this poem are the loss of a loved one and, perhaps, love itself. The lines that say *"Erias hath sheathed this sword long, long ago"* tell us that Gorias was abandoned in the far distant past and its guardian no longer needs to stand vigilant. This would imply that access to Gorias would be unhindered but, after reading the sorrow of this and the other poems, you must begin to ask yourself do I really want to go there? Let's see what Fiona had to say about the last city.

Murias

In the sunken city of Murias
A golden Image dwells:
The sea-song of the trampling waves
Is as muffled bells
Where He dwells,
In the city of Murias.

In the sunken city of Murias
A golden Image gleams:
The loud noise of the moving seas
Is as woven beams
Where He dreams,
In the city of Murias.

In the sunken city of Murias,
Deep, deep beneath the sea
The Image sits and hears Time break
The heart I gave to thee
And thou to me,
In the city of Murias.

In the city of Murias,
Long, oh, so long ago,
Our souls were wed when the world
was young;
And we old now, that we know
This silent woe
In the city of Murias?

In the sunken city of Murias
A graven Image dwells:
The sound of our little sobbing prayer
Is as muffled bells
Where He dwells,
In the city of Murias.

This is the only one of the four Faery poems where the guardian of the city is not referred to by name. Instead Fiona uses the pronoun 'he' but note that it is always given in Upper Case, 'He,' a convention normally reserved only for deity or royalty. According to the Gaelic version his name is Semias. This may be the Faery version of the very similar name known in our world as Seumas. This is very interesting when we consider that it was the old Hebridean fisherman Seumas Macleod who taught William Sharp much Gaelic lore in his childhood. See Chapter Five for a full discussion on this.

I discuss in detail in my book *The Little Book of the Great Enchantment* the probability that Seumas Macleod was the father of the Faery Fiona Macleod. This may explain why Fiona does not specifically name him in her poem and it may also explain the use of the upper case pronoun. The subject of this poem, the Faery city of Murias, is closely connected with the sea and water in general. Seumas Macleod was a fisherman and whenever either William Sharp or Fiona Macleod spoke of him it was always in connection with, or in proximity to, the sea. Throughout her life, albeit a life that was lived through William Sharp, Fiona was intensely private and never publicly discussed much about herself, family or upbringing at all. If, as I believe, these poems on the four cities are autobiographical then her reticence at specifically identifying her own father fits the normal pattern of her life. This may also explain the reference in verse four to souls being wed which could be a cryptic reference to her father Seumas 'coupling' with Edith Wingate Rinder to produce the Faery being Fiona Macleod, the author of these poems. I discuss in detail this whole fascinating aspect of Fiona Macleod's life in my biography of William Sharp and mention it here for the benefit of readers unfamiliar with the paternity of Fiona Macleod.

On a literary note, when this poem appeared in the United States in the Thomas B. Mosher reprint of Fiona's book *From The Hills of Dream* it was called *Requiem* and appeared without the other three dirges. It is clearly a poem that held deep personal significance for Fiona.

So, to return to the question posed above, is the purpose of these poems to warn us to keep away from these deserted Faery cities? I would now answer – no. If they have any inherent warning message it is more one of 'be prepared' rather than one of 'don't come.' But their purpose is two-fold. They are intended to inform us of the existence of these Faery cities in the first place and, secondly, to make their imagery available to us so that we can go there, at least in the visual imagination, as an entry point to the broader Realm of Faery. The warning is more 'don't linger too long' rather than a flat-out 'don't come.'

Some supplemental symbolism is appropriate here. Fiona referred to the Four Coloured Winds throughout her writings and both she and William also gave many other connections between the four directions of space and many other things. These other associations, via their connections with the four directions, can be connected with the Four Cities as well. For example, one of William's personal notebooks contains the following entry:

Angus of the Four Keys

The East: Birth: The Key of Music   *E*
The South: War: The Key of Passion   *S*
The West: Dreams: The Key of Sorrow   *W*
The North: Life: The Key of Death   *N*

The Key of the East, that is also the Key of Birth, and the Key of Music
The Key of the South, that is also the Key of War, and the Key of Passion
The Key of the West, that is also the Key of Dreams, and the Key of Sorrow
The Key of the North, that is also the Key of Life, and the Key of Death

This list of associations appeared in a slightly different form in Fiona's important play *The Immortal Hour*. Note though that although the first four lines agree with the entry in William's notebook and likewise attribute ownership of these Four Keys to the god Angus (given below in its Irish spelling), the final three lines imply that there is a fifth key which is owned by Dalua:

Other Voices   *Oengus, keeper of the East: of Birth: of Song:*
                    The keeper of the South: of Passion: and of War:
                    The keeper of the West: of Sorrow: of Dreams:
                    The keeper of the North: of Death: of Life.

Dalua   *Yet one more ancient even than the god of the sun,*
Than flame-haired Oengus, lord of Love and Death,
Holds the last dreadful key … Oblivion.

Fiona's essay *The Divine Adventure* reveals even more connections with these Fours:

Wind comes from the spring star in the east; fire from the summer star in the south; water from the autumn star in the west; wisdom, silence and death from the star in the north.

Note that only three seasons are named. Winter is not mentioned at all. This is consistent with the early Celtic view of the world and the passing of the seasons.

Yet another reference to the Fours is said to have been given to William by his old Gaelic nurse Barbara. The first two words on each line are the Gaelic names for the star, and its direction as shown in parentheses following.

The Four Stars of Destiny

Reul Near (Star of the East), Give us kindly birth;
Reul Deas (Star of the South), Give us great love;
Reul Siar (Star of the West), Give us great age;
Reul Tuath (Star of the North), Give us Death.

Finally, William's friend and magical collaborator William Butler Yeats came up with an association concerning the Four Directions and four species of trees. I have never seen this particular grouping anywhere else and unfortunately Yeats did not say where he got it. But, for the sake of completeness, I give it here,

Apple in the East
Rowan in the South
Oak in the North
Hazel in the West

I would strongly suggest however that the excited and eager traveller to the Realm of Faery should really study, think about, and digest the deeper aspects of the imagery used in these poems before setting off, and most important of all, link all this Faery imagery to that of the Glen of Precious Stones as described in *The Chronicles of the Sidhe* where it is said, *"They had four cities at the four ends of the green diamond that is the world. That in the north was made of earth; that in the east, of air; that in the south, of fire; that in the west, of water. In the middle of the green diamond that is the world is the Glen of Precious Stones. It is in the shape of a heart, and glows like a ruby, though all stones and gems are there. It is there that the Sidhe go to refresh their deathless life."* The four cities should be used as an entry point, as doorways if you like, into the much more important Glen of Precious Stones. In other words, don't stand in the doorway, don't block up the hall – move on to the place you have really come to see and experience, the Glen of Precious Stones.

A final group of fours comes from Fiona's *The Laughter of Peterkin*, her only book written specifically for children. In the prologue to this tale there is a section concerning the young child Peterkin which is in fact autobiographical and taken from the early life of William Sharp. We are told that one moonlit night Peterkin sneaked out of his bedroom to watch the fairies playing around a great white poplar tree, and the section concludes with,

"In those first fragments of Peterkin's experiences, all his life was foreshadowed. Wonder, delight, longing, laughter — the four winds of childhood — these blew for him through his first few years, through childhood and boyhood and youth. He is a man now; but though the laughter is rarer and the longing deeper and more constant, there still blow through the dark glens and wide sunlit moors of his mind the four winds of Laughter, Longing, Wonder, and Delight."

In Chapter Eleven I give an excerpt from my notebooks on some personal practical magical work I had been carrying out on the Scottish Isle of Iona some years ago, in order to show the reader the manner in which Faery communication can sometimes work. Now, to answer the paradox posed in Chapter Three concerning whether or not it is possible to use the Four Elements of the physical world while working magically in the non-physical realm of Faery, I give below a further excerpt from my magical notebooks at that time dealing with the problem of attributing a physical world Element to each of the Realm of Faery Four Cities. This is taken more or less verbatim from my notebooks with only some minor changes for grammatical and clarification purposes.

I was attempting to understand some vague ideas I had been given from the Realm of Faery concerning a totally new way of working ritual magic involving a pyramid made of four equilateral triangles, i.e. with a triangular base and three sides as opposed to the familiar Egyptian pyramid with a square base and four sides. I was using as a focus the mound of rock and earth that sits facing the entrance to the abbey on the Isle of Iona because I had suddenly noticed for the first time the obvious fact that it is more or less in the shape of just such a triangular pyramid. At the apex of this mound there is a large slot in the ground, the purpose of which is explained in Chapter Eleven. My notes for what happened that day say:

> *The significance and symbolism of the three dimensional pyramid is extremely important. Any ritual based on this whole abstract concept must have four participants – three of whom stand at the points of the base triangle of the pyramid and the fourth is at the apex. I struggled for a long time to figure out how exactly this can be accomplished in a formal ritual setting. I had automatically been assuming that this new, strange ritual would be performed indoors in a formal temple or lodge setting and I could not see how this could be achieved in practice in the two dimensions of the horizontal lodge floor. That is where the problem was. This was clearly not suited to such an indoor setting so why not see if it might work outdoors. Then it became obvious – three Officers can stand equidistant around the base of the mound and the fourth stand atop. This suddenly felt right; I was on the right track. I also realised that as well as this important little pyramid-shaped mound in Iona there are many others on a much larger scale scattered around, such as Glastonbury Tor and Saint Michael's Mount in Cornwall, or Mont St. Michel in France, all of which are deemed 'sacred' and all of which can be used in the manner that follows.*

> *With this realisation of how a three-sided pyramid can be used magically by the traditional Four Officers I then saw how the Four Cities, and therefore the Four Elements can be coordinated with the four points of the pyramid – three on the base and one on the top. Again this felt very much like I was finally on the right track. The next realisation that suddenly came to me was that the allocation of a City to a point on the pyramid can <u>and should</u> be done on a <u>rotating</u> basis each time this type of ritual is worked. Here is another new and radical concept! This*

idea of rotation seemed very apt because no matter which way you place the pyramid it is always the same shape with three equidistant horizontal points all of which are also equidistant from the highest point. You therefore cannot allocate the Four Cities to one specific and permanent point in the same way that you can allocate the Four Quarters and the Four Elements to a specific fixed Quarter in the normal, two-dimensional structure of a regular magical ritual. The addition of the fourth point on the apex of the pyramid, above the triangular base, allows for a much greater deal of fluidity and flexibility than the simple flat horizontal four-fold layout of a conventional magical working space. This all now started to make a great deal of sense and provide a degree of clarity I had not had before, concerning how the Four Elements of this world can relate to the Four Cities of the realm of Faery and how these can be used together in successful magical rituals. The key is to realise that the fixed, set and immovable allocation of these 'fours' is fine in the physical world but they must be understood to be movable and changeable in the non-physical realm of Faery.

This led on to one more important realisation concerning the magical Faery pyramid. In any traditional magical working a sacred space is defined and drawn and the four directions, with appropriate symbolism, are opened. The crucial point in such a ritual is that everything that follows is done <u>within</u> this limited sacred space. Any movements of the performing Officers are made within this space; any higher-level contacts that are made are brought within the sacred space etc. It is all carried out within a clearly defined limited area. The Faery pyramid style of magical working though is exactly the opposite — everything that is done by the Four Officers is projected <u>outwards</u> along the lines of the pyramid's four intersecting points and out into the world, both human and Faery.

It is important to realise and understand these radical and fundamental differences between the human way of working magic and the Faery way. These differences are so great that any attempt to work a normal Western Mystery Tradition or Wiccan ritual within the pyramid simply cannot work and could lead to a lot of difficulty for the magician. But accepting the fluidity and mobility of the magical symbols and attributions within the Faery tradition brings with it an increased sense of potential and possibility.

Chapter Ten

Joy and Sorrow

I have gone out and seen the lands of Faery
And have found sorrow and peace and beauty there,
And have not known one from the other,
But found each
Lovely and gracious alike, delicate and fair.

MUCH OF THE Faery lore given out by Fiona deals with abstract concepts and connections that are unrecognized or, at best, poorly understood in our limited human outlook. Consequently it proved difficult for her to express her message simply and in a way we could readily grasp and understand. Some of these concepts took a whole story to put across or had to be repeated several times in various ways in the rest of her writings, in an effort for their importance to be seen and recognised by those who can see more than just the romantic ramblings of a Victorian gentlewoman. Because these new concepts had no pre-existing vocabulary in our world she was restricted to using words and phrases that were close to what she had to say but were not necessarily accurate. This has understandably caused some of her more important points to be missed even by the few people who have made a consistent effort to untangle her Faery lore.

A clue to identifying these important passages is to look for repeated words or phrases that occur throughout her books, especially when repeated throughout a story or poem, or when used in quick succession. One example is her frequent use of the words 'joy' and 'sorrow'. As well as paying attention to the occurrence of these actual words it is also important to note that occasionally she put across her same message without using these two words but instead by describing joyous, happy events that quickly, and unexpectedly, turn to tragedy and sorrow.

This theme, of course, is common to literature throughout human history and across all cultures, but the important Faery lore she was so keen to pass on deals with harnessing and utilizing the emotions that both joy and sorrow invoke. This is an aspect of the Faery Tradition that has no real direct equivalent in the world of humankind. Certainly throughout human history there have been countless stories, poems, songs and plays that deal with the overall theme of joy becoming sorrow, of sorrow becoming joy, and of how people deal with and overcome these abrupt and drastic changes in circumstances. Almost every love story ever written brings in one or both of these swings from joy to sorrow to joy once more. But Fiona's message is much more than this. It tells us to be aware of these emotions in the moment and to understand that the energy they contain can be used to consciously shape what is happening in that moment. If you read her works with this topic in mind you will notice how very often joy and sorrow come into her tales, and not just in her romances where it is to be expected, but also in her many other stories and essays that deal with every other human emotion and situation. She was trying to give us examples over and over again, in different circumstances, with different characters and with different plots and vignettes, to make us aware of the deeper spiritual truths behind joy and sorrow.

However, it has to be pointed out that experiencing joy and sorrow consciously at a deep spiritual level does not negate or distance these emotions and feelings, nor does it lessen their impact on the daily life of the individual in the physical world. In the case of joy this may actually be welcomed and encouraged by the seeker after deeper knowledge – what's wrong with intensifying the level of joy? But it must be remembered that sorrow will be similarly intensified and may become overwhelming and crushing to the individual who is trying to cope with not just the normal, day-to-day emotional upset caused by sorrow but also the increased intensity that a spiritual awareness of sorrow brings. This is no light matter.

If we shift our focus away from Fiona's written output for a moment and take a look at the personal, day-to-day life she lived through William Sharp we can see this theme of intensified joy and sorrow playing out over and over again in the real world events that shaped William's short life on this earth. This is a clear, well-documented case of what can happen when humans and Faeries develop strong connections and when the human partner starts to grapple with the Faery understanding of joy and sorrow. Throughout his life William Sharp was frequently described by friends and acquaintances as being a very social, flamboyant person who at times was quite mischievous and childlike in a fun, playful way. But he also suffered periods of deep depression to the point at one time he was under a suicide watch by his wife, doctor and friends. This is of course an extreme example and was caused by the fact that he was working with the Faery Fiona Macleod in a relationship that was closer and deeper than any of us is ever likely to experience. But it serves to remind us that by bringing the Faery Tradition through the veil and into our human world we open ourselves up to new and powerful emotional changes and challenges. And these are not necessarily pleasant, wonderful or satisfying. We must exercise caution and restraint in these matters but they have much to teach us and they should not be shied away from completely.

In 1899 while William Sharp was suffering from depression and struggling with the trivia of daily life, Fiona commented in a letter to an admirer:

"... though young in years, I have a capacity for sorrow and regret which has come to me through my Celtic ancestry out of a remote lost world: because, indeed, I have myself walked the blind way between Joy and Sorrow and been led now by the one and now by the other. But do not think I am a melancholy person. I am not."

This clearly shows that such moving between joy and sorrow is a normal thing where she comes from and that it brings neither permanent depression nor on-going elation. This is rarely the case in our world and is yet another example of the subtle but important differences between our world and the Realm of Faery.

The important part of her comment is, *"I have myself walked the blind way between Joy and Sorrow and been led now by the one and now by the other."* This lets us know that the individual must submit and allow joy and sorrow to take the lead, to walk *'the blind way'* trusting that joy and sorrow will be true and faithful guides. The image this invokes for me is of a long, winding road stretching before me with distractions on either side that attract my attention for a moment and then are gone when the next distraction happens along. If I visualize joy being on one side of the road and sorrow on the other then I can see clearly how I am still walking forward under my own will but every now and then – not constantly, this is important – my attention is grabbed by something to my left or right that causes me either joy or sorrow, but as I continue to walk ever forward that distraction fades as it becomes more and more distant. There may then follow a period of equilibrium when neither joy nor sorrow is dominant. But inevitably another distraction will come along. Keeping this in mind helps me to remember during times of sorrow that I am still progressing forward under my own will and that this difficult time will pass.

But, I hear you say, what of the joyous times? Are they too going to fade and disappear into the background as you walk along? The answer is a clear yes, of course they are, but others will replace them as you walk onwards, and you will always have your memories of those joyful times even as they fade and die. Many people in this world who are melancholy or depressed have not learned to enjoy the joy of the moment and then let it go when it naturally fades and is gone. Always looking back to happy times that are gone means you are not looking forward along the road that winds through joy and sorrow. In such a state you will experience neither real joy nor real sorrow any more. All your apparent experiences will be no more than the fantasies and ramblings of your own mind. Let go of these imaginations and stretch out your open hands once more to the real guides through life, Joy and Sorrow.

Perhaps the most obvious real-life example of joy and sorrow manifesting in Fiona's life at a higher, more significant level, involves Dr. John Arthur Goodchild. In the late 1890s Fiona started a correspondence that would last for several years with this Dr. Goodchild. He was an English doctor who spent the winters in Italy tending to the medical needs of the many British who spent the winters in the Mediterranean climate away from the cold and smog of the big British cities. He was an amateur archaeologist, writer and a bit of a mystic. While in Italy he came across an ancient glass bowl that would herald a revival of the Grail Mysteries in Britain, and started quite a sensation. For full details of Dr. Goodchild and his bowl see my book *The Little Book of the Great Enchantment* and Patrick Benham's excellent book *The Avalonians*. For the time being it is sufficient to know that Goodchild was in sympathy with the thoughts, ideas and beliefs that Fiona had been making public in her writings, and she in turn felt that he was an ally with whom she could be more open and frank in her letters. Goodchild did not know that he was actually dealing with William Sharp.

I do not know if Goodchild was aware of his own strong intuitive powers but he certainly had them, and much of his correspondence displays some remarkably intuitive comments and predictions. In 1904, after several years of corresponding, he and William Sharp met for the first time and the events that followed that day are of importance to anyone looking for an understanding of the Faery Tradition as revealed by Fiona Macleod.

It was on Monday August 1st 1904, a Bank Holiday in England, and coincidentally the ancient Celtic festival of Lughnasadh, that William and Goodchild met in Glastonbury. Unknown to William, Goodchild had decided to apply a psychic test on his friend. He had decided that if William should use the word 'joy' during their time together in Glastonbury it would be a sign that he could confide in him the secret of his ancient glass bowl, of which at that time William knew nothing. Later William described what happened in a letter to a friend.

"As usual one or two strange things happened in connection with Dr. G. We went across the ancient 'Salmon' of St. Bride, which stretches below the hill known as 'Weary-All' (a corruption of Uriel, the Angel of the Sun), and about a mile or less westward came upon the narrow water of the ancient 'Burgh'. Near here is a very old Thorn held in great respect. He put me (unknowing) to a singular test. He had hoped with especial and deep hope that in some significant way I would write or utter the word 'Joy' on this first day of August... – and also to see if certain spiritual influence would reach me. Well, later in the day (for he could not prompt or suggest, and had to await occurrence) we went into the lovely grounds of the ancient ruined Abbey, one of the loveliest things in England I think. I became restless and left him, and went and lay down behind an angle of the east end, under the tree. I smoked, and then rested idly, and then began thinking of some correspondence I had forgotten. Suddenly I turned on my right side, stared at the broken stone of the angle, and felt vaguely moved in some way. Abruptly and unpremeditatedly I wrote down three enigmatic and disconnected lines. I was looking curiously at the third when I saw Dr. G approach. 'Can you make anything of that,' I said – 'I've just written it, I don't know why.' This is the triad:

'From the Silence of Time, Time's Silence Borrow.
In the heart of To-day is the word of To-morrow.
The Builders of Joy are the Children of Sorrow.'"

Needless to say, Goodchild was delighted. Not only had William used the word 'joy' but also the word 'sorrow.' This not only proved William had passed the psychic test with flying colours but also confirmed a suspicion Goodchild had had that the fate of the bowl, which he saw as a 'Cup of Sorrow,' was for it to be transformed into a 'Cup of Joy.' Fiona later took William's little verse, expanded it, and used it as the fore piece to her book *Bride of the Isles*. This longer version reads,

I
From the silence of Time, Time's silence borrow:
This is the Ancient Wisdom of Patience.
Patience – Silence – Stars of the Dusk of the Spirit.

II
In the heart of To-day is the word of To-morrow –
As Twilight sleeps in the noon and ariseth at Even,
As the Wave of Midnight uplifteth the Star of the Morning.

III
The Builders of Joy are the Children of Sorrow.
Bitter the waters of Grief; but sweet is the Well Spring.
Stoop and be fearless: drink, O ye Builders of Joy.

The last line is significant, *"Stoop and be fearless: drink..."* is clearly saying do not fear the waters of Grief, they will inevitably bring Joy. Go ahead and embrace grief and sorrow in the knowledge that they will not last. All that is required is a change in attitude, in outlook, regarding the real nature of sorrow. You will never be able to avoid it. Instead, accept it when it appears and see it for what it truly is – energy of transformation that is neither good nor bad, negative nor positive.

Several years after the Glastonbury meeting, many people started to consider Goodchild's bowl to be nothing less than the Holy Grail. It came into the possession of three young women who would care for it on Goodchild's behalf and they composed several rituals and ceremonies that were used in spiritual services in honour of what they believed to be the Grail. One of these new rituals included the lines, *"Hail Cup of Joy! ... Bless me that I may be an instrument fitted for the holy work of turning the Cup of Sorrow into the Cup of Joy."* The Irish poet and mystic William Butler Yeats, also a long term correspondent and confidante of Fiona's, would later incorporate this image of sorrow becoming joy in one of the rituals created for his secret occult group known as the Celtic Mystical Order. Part of one of this group's rituals, the Initiation of the Fiery Spear, says, *"The Child of the Cauldron received in Sorrow, is brought forth and becomes the Child of the Spear in Joy."*

Goodchild was so influential to Fiona that she dedicated her book *The Winged Destiny* to him. Part of this dedication says:

> *"You who know the way of the wind in my mind know that I do not, as some say, 'dwell only in the past,' or that personal sorrow is the one magnet of my dreams. It is not the night-wind in sad hearts only that I hear, or the sighing of vain futilities; but, often, rather an emotion akin to that mysterious Sorrow of Eternity in love with tears ... It is, at times at least I feel it so, because Beauty is more beautiful there. It is the twilight hour in the heart, as Joy is the heart's morning ... Music, like the rose of the Greeks, is 'the thirty petalled one,' and every leaf is the gate of an equal excellence. The fragrance of all is Joy, the beauty of all is Sorrow: but the Rose is one — 'Rosa Sempiterna,' the Rose of Life."*

Here Fiona is pointing out how beauty is intensified when seen through the eyes and a heart that are filled with sorrow. Remembering that beauty is synonymous with the Realm of Faery gives this an even deeper meaning. Often the sorrow overshadows this beautification and we miss it, but nonetheless it is there. Learning to keep this in mind while experiencing sorrow is not easy, but it is an integral part of the practical aspect of Faery magic. Fiona follows this comment by reminding us that sorrow and joy are part and parcel of each other and inseparable components in the make-up of life itself.

The Winged Destiny also contains an essay entitled *The Gaelic Heart*, part of which says:

> *"One must with the lantern of the spirit look into the dark troubled water of the Gaelic heart, too, I think, if one would understand. How else can one understand the joy that is so near to sorrow, the sorrow that like the wave of the sea can break in a moment into light and beauty? I have heard often in effect, 'This is no deep heart that in one hour weeps and in the next laughs.' But I know a deeper heart that in one hour weeps and in the next laughs, so deep that light dies away within it, and silence and the beginning and the end are one: the heart of the sea. And there is another heart that is deep, and weeps one hour and in the next laughs; the heart of Night... where Oblivion smiles, and it is day; sighs, and the darkness is*

come. And there is another heart that is deep, and weeps in one hour and in the next laughs: the soul of man: where tears and laughter are the fans that blow the rose-white flame of life. And I am well content that the Gaelic heart, that in one hour weeps and in the next laughs, though it be so sad and worn among smiling nations, is in accord with the great spirits of the world and with immortal things."

Note the strong reference to the sea in this context. I have commented elsewhere in this book on the importance of water and the sea. I have also previously commented on how the word Gaelic in Fiona's writings is interchangeable with Faery, and that 'deep' is a metaphor for the Realm of Faery. Knowing this helps reveal a deeper level of meaning to the above quotation.

Here again Fiona is stressing that sorrow and joy are conjoined and one will quickly become the other. This is a natural and necessary thing. The Gaelic/Faery heart has learned to switch quickly between them in a way that heightens the experience of both, and in a way that leads life further down the road of fulfilment. The opening sentences are addressing the fact that in our everyday human world it is considered odd or even abnormal for a person to be seen to be willing to accept sorrow and to switch between periods of intense sorrow and intense joy with apparent ease. Fiona is pointing out that she regards this to be a much more common and healthy phenomenon than most people care to admit. It is not surprising that most people today shun sorrow when they are constantly being told, even if only subliminally, that the 'pursuit of happiness' is their one true goal and birthright. Nobody ever speaks of the pursuit of happiness *and sorrow*. Sorrow, the twin sibling of joy, has been pushed out of the picture to the point that it is considered a wise and sensible thing to seek counselling or therapy during periods of intense sorrow but nobody is encouraged to seek 'help' when they are overjoyed.

Another important person in the lives of William Sharp and Fiona Macleod, although for very different and deeply personal reasons, was his illegitimate daughter Esther Mona who was born in 1901. William knew that he would never be able to be a close father to her and that he would probably not live long enough to see her grow and mature – on both of these counts he was right – so Fiona left her a message across time. In the Thomas B. Mosher American printing of *Deirdre and the Sons of Usna* there is a lengthy, deeply moving dedication to Esther Mona that in part says:

"Long ago, one of the old forgotten gods, the god of enchantment and illusion, made a glory that was a glory of loveliness, an ecstasy of sound, and a passion of delight. Then he watched seven mortals approach it. Three saw in it no loveliness, heard in it no ecstasy, caught from it no rapture. Of three others, one knew an inexplicable delight, and took away the wonder and memory to be his while he lived: and one heard an ecstasy of sound, and went away rapt, and forgetting all things because of that dream and passion not seen but heard: and the third looked on that loveliness, and ever after his fellows spoke of him as one made insane by impossible dreams, though he had that in his life which rose in a white flame, and quenched his thirst at the wells of the spirit, and rejoiced continually. But of the seven only one saw the glory as the god of enchantment and illusion had made it, seeing in it the spirit that is Beauty, and hearing in it the soul of Music, and uplifted by it to the rapture that is the passion of delight. And lest that evil Destiny that puts dust upon dreams, and silence upon sweet airs, and stills songs, and makes the hand idle, and the mind an eddying leaf, and the spirit as foam upon the sea, should take from this dreamer what he had won, the god of enchantment and illusion gave the man a broken heart, and a mind filled with the sighing of weariness, and sorrow to be his secret friend and the silence upon his pillow by night.

And I have told you this to help you to understand that it is what we bring to the enchantment that matters more than what the enchantment may disclose. And, when you have been kissed by sorrow — may the darker veiled Dread pass you, dear — you will understand why the seventh dreamer who looked upon the secret wonder was of the few whom the gods touch with the hands, of the chosen keepers and guardians of the immortal fire."

The first paragraph could fall under the heading of 'the mythology of Faery' as it relates a Faery legend concerning the coming into being of joy and sorrow. The reference to *"one of the old forgotten gods, the god of enchantment and illusion"* is to the Faery god Dalua. In most Faery legends Dalua is connected with madness and the bringing of death. It therefore seems very uncharacteristic of him to create *"a glory of loveliness, an ecstasy of sound, and a passion of delight"* – all things that appear to be the polar opposite of his normal attributions. This, though, once again points out that the apparently 'negative' aspects of Dalua must be balanced with the 'positive' things such as those he caused to be manifest. He cannot exist without both negative and positive, sorrow and joy, any more than anyone else can, human or Faery.

The following sentences then relate how seven individuals reacted very differently to discovering this intensely positive, joyful scene. Their individual reactions are exactly the same ones that are manifest today when people are exposed to an intensity of either joy or sorrow. Some show no reaction at all, others find some little aspect of joy or sorrow that they latch onto while ignoring the rest, yet other people can see much more into the joy or sorrow but this insight overwhelms them to the point of losing their grasp on the realities of this world. All of these unhealthy reactions are caused by the simple fact that they are all focused on either total joy, as in this case, or total sorrow, to the complete exclusion of the other. This imbalance is unhealthy because it is unnatural. Dalua knows this and sees that only one of the seven has grasped that what he is looking at would be totally fulfilling if only it was complete, so to correct this Dalua, *"gave the man a broken heart, and a mind filled with the sighing of weariness, and sorrow to be his secret friend and the silence upon his pillow by night."* In other words Dalua allows the seventh individual to experience joy to its fullest by giving him sorrow as 'his secret friend' and the peace of mind that is 'the silence upon his pillow by night.' This is all summed up in the last short paragraph: *"when you have been kissed by sorrow… you will understand why the seventh dreamer who looked upon the secret wonder was of the few whom the gods touch with the hands, of the chosen keepers and guardians of the immortal fire."*

The first sentence of the last paragraph makes the important point that *"it is what we bring to the enchantment that matters more than what the enchantment may disclose."* The seventh individual had no preconceptions and brought an open mind to the experience. Because of this she was able to see past the great joy that was presented to her and realise that it was incomplete and out of balance. Keeping in mind that Fiona used the word 'enchantment' to mean the Realm of Faery we can now see that this is a clear and important message concerning the practical aspects of approaching the Realm of Faery. Don't go there with expectations and anticipations. Go there for a reason, with a purpose, but do not try to determine the outcome of your visit before you even get there. When you are presented with something or someone unexpected or mysterious (as is often the case) remember the seventh individual – approach it with an open mind and return with what *the Faeries want you to take away* not what *you think* you should be taking away.

In her essay *Iona* Fiona relates the tale of how an old horse belonging to the monks on Iona knew that St. Columba's death was near. In a very touching scene she describes the old white horse nuzzle into the old, white-haired saint and shed great tears because it knew Columba would soon be departing this life. One of the young monks saw this and tried to chase the horse away but Columba told the monk to leave him be for the horse knew more than the young monk would ever know. Following this well-known tale from the life of St. Columba Fiona says:

> *"If there be any to whom the aged Colum comforting the grief of his old white pony is a matter of disdain or derision, I would not have his soul in exchange for the dumb sorrow of that creature. One would fare further with that sorrow, though soulless, than with the soul that could not understand that sorrow."*

This requires no further comment from me.

So important is this understanding of joy and sorrow that Fiona used it as the theme for many of her poems. One of the most specific poems on the subject is,

Mater Consolatrix

Heart's-joy must fade ... though it borrow
Heaven's azure for its clay:
But the Joy that is one with Sorrow,
Treads an immortal way,
For each, is born To-morrow,
For each, is Yesterday.

Joy that is clothed with shadow
Shall arise from the dead:
But Joy that is clothed with the rainbow
Shall with the bow be sped: ...
Where the Sun spends his fires is she,
And where the Stars are led.

Fiona's first publication, the novel *Pharais*, is based on a whole series of happy and tragic events that show time and time again the importance of understanding the deeper energies that are flowing through these events. In this book she also linked joy and sorrow, but especially sorrow, to the lot of Womankind, a subject that she tackled frequently. This is summed up in a lengthy poem from *Pharais* called:

The Prayer of Women

O spirit that broods upon the hills
And moves upon the face of the deep,
And is heard in the wind,
Save us from the desire of men's eyes,
And the cruel lust of them.
Save us from the springing of the cruel seed
In that narrow house which is as the grave
For darkness and loneliness ...
That women carry with them with shame, and
Weariness, and long pain,
Only for the laughter of man's heart,
And for the joy that triumphs therein,
And the sport that is in the heart.
Wherewith he mocketh us,
Wherewith he playeth with us,
Wherewith he trampleth upon us ...
Us, who conceive and bear him;
Us, who bring him forth;
Who feed him in the womb, and at the breast, and at the knee:
Whom he calleth Mother,
And Mother again of his wife and children:
When he looks at our hair and sees that it is white;
And at our eyes and sees they are dim;
And at our lips straightened out with long pain;
And at our breasts, fallen and seared as a barren hill;
And at our hands, worn with toil;
And, seeing, seeth all the bitter ruin and wreck of us —
All save the violated womb that curses him —
All save the heart that forebeareth ... for pity —
All save the living brain that condemneth him —
All save the spirit that shall not mate with him —
All save the soul he shall never see
Till he be one with it, and equal;
He who hath the bridle, but guideth not;
He who hath the whip, yet is driven;
He who as a shepherd calleth upon us,
But is himself a lost sheep, crying among the hills!

O Spirit, and the Nine Angels who watch us,
And Thy Son, and Mary Virgin,
Heal us of the wrong of man:
We whose breasts are weary with milk,
Cry, cry to Thee, O Compassionate!

Fiona wrote several other long poems on the theme of the sorrow of Woman. Elizabeth Sharp, William's widow, collected them together and reprinted them in the *Collected Works of Fiona Macleod, Volume VII: Poems and Dramas*. I reproduce them here in their entirety for they contain a great deal of valuable insight and Faery spiritual belief.

The Rune of the Passion of Woman

We who love are those who suffer,
We who suffer most are those who most do love.
O the heartbreak come of longing love,
O the heartbreak come of love deferred,
O the heartbreak of love grown listless.
Far upon the lonely hills I have heard the crying,
The lamentable crying of the ewes,
And dreamed I heard the sorrow of poor mothers
Made lambless too and weary with that sorrow:
And far away upon the waves I have heard the crying,
The lamentable cry of the seamews,
And dreamed I heard the wailing of the women
Whose hearts are flamed with love above the gravestone,
Whose hearts beat fast but hear no fellow-beating.
Bitter, alas, the sorrow of lonely women,
When no man by the ingle sits, and in the cradle
No little flower-like faces flush with slumber:
Bitter the loss of these, the lonely silence,
The bed void, the hearthside void,
The void heart and only the grave not void:
But bitterer, oh more bitter still, the longing
Of women who have known no love at all,
Who never,
Never, never have grown hot and cold with rapture
'Neath the lips or 'neath the clasp of longing,
Who have never opened eyes of heaven to man's devotion,

Joy and Sorrow

Who have never heard a husband whisper "wife,"
Who have lost their youth, their dreams, their fairness,
In a vain upgrowing to a light that comes not.
Bitter these: but bitterer than either,
O most bitter for the heart of woman
To have loved and been loved with passion,
To have known the height and depth, the vision
Of triple-flaming love — and in the heart-self
Sung a song of deathless love, immortal,
Sunrise-haired, and starry-eyed and wondrous:
To have felt the brain sustain the mighty
Weight and reach of thought unspanned and spanless,
To have felt the soul grow large and noble,
To have felt the spirit dauntless, eager, swift in hope and daring,
To have felt the body grow in fairness,
And the glory and the beauty of the body
Thrill with joy of living, feel the bosom
Rise and fall with sudden tides of passion,
Feel the lift of soul to soul, and know the rapture
Of the rising triumph of the ultimate dream
Beyond the pale place of defeated dreams:
To know all this, to feel all this, to be a woman
Crowned with the double crown of lily and rose
And have the morning star to rule the golden hours
And have the evening start thro' hours of dream,
To live, to do, to act, to dream, to hope,
To be a perfect woman with the full
Sweet, wondrous and consummate joy
Of womanhood fulfilled to all desire —
And then ... oh then, to know the waning of the vision,
To go through days and nights of starless longing,
Through nights and days of gloom and bitter sorrow:
To see the fairness of the body passing,
To see the beauty wither, the sweet colour
Fade, the coming of the wintry lines
Upon pale faces chilled with idle loving,
The slow subsidence of the tides of living.
To feel all this, and know the desolate sorrow
Of the pale place of all defeated dreams,

And to cry out with aching lips, and vainly;
And to cry out with aching heart, and vainly;
And to cry out with aching brain, and vainly;
And to cry out with aching soul, and vainly;
To cry, cry, cry with passionate heartbreak, sobbing,
To the dim wondrous shape of Love retreating —
To grope blindly for the warm hand, the swift touch,
To seek blindly for the starry lamps of passion,
To crave blindly for the dear words of longing!
To go forth cold, and dreary, and lonely, O so lonely,
With the heart-cry even as the crying,
The lamentable crying on the hills
When lambless ewes go desolately astray —
Yes, to go forth discrowned at last, who have worn
The flower-sweet lovely crown of rapturous love:
To know the eyes have lost their starry wonder;
To know the hair no more a fragrant dusk
Wherein to whisper secrets of deep longing;
To know the breasts shall henceforth be no haven
For the dear weary head that loved to lie there —
To go, to know, and yet to live and suffer,
To be as use and wont demand, to fly no signal
That the soul founders in a sea of sorrow,
But to be "true," "a woman," "patient," "tender,"
"Divinely acquiescent," all-forbearing,
To laugh, and smile, to comfort, to sustain,
To do all this — oh this is the bitterest,
O this the heaviest cross, O this the tree
Whereon the woman hath her crucifixion.

But, O ye women, what avail? Behold,
Men worship at the tree, whereon it is writ
The legend of the broken hearts of women.
And this is the end: for young and old the end:
For fair and sweet, for those not sweet nor fair,
For loved, unloved and those who once were loved,
For all the women of all this weary world
Of joy too brief and sorrow far too long,
This is the end: the cross, the bitter tree,

And worship of the phantom raised on high
Out of your love, your passion, your despair,
Hopes unfulfilled, and unavailing tears.

The Rune of the Sorrow of Women

This is the rune of the women who bear in sorrow:
Who, having anguish of body, die in the pangs of bearing,
Who, with the ebb at the heart, pass ere the wane of the babe-mouth.

THE RUNE

O we are tired, we are tired, all we who are women:
Heavy the breasts with milk that never shall nourish:
Heavy the womb that never again shall be weighty.
For we have the burthen upon us, we have the burthen,
The long slow pain, the sorrow of going, and the parting.
O little hands, O little lips, farewell and farewell.
Bitter the sorrow of bearing only to end with the parting.

THE DREAM

Far away in the east of the world a woman had sorrow.
Heavy she was with child, and the pains were upon her.
And God looked forth out of heaven, and he spake in his pity:
"O Mary, thou bearest the Prince of Peace,
and thy seed shall be blessed."
But Mary the Mother sighed, and God the All-Seeing wondered,
For this is the rune he heard in the heart of Mary the Virgin:—
"Man blindfold soweth the seed, and blindly he reapeth:
And to the word of the Lord is a blessing upon the sower.
O what of the blessing upon the field that is sown,
What of the sown, not of the sower, what of the mother, the bearer?
Sure it is this that I see: that everywhere over the world
The man has the pain and the sorrow, the weary womb and the travail!
Everywhere patient he is, restraining the tears of his patience

Slow in upbraiding, swift in passion unselfish,
Bearing his pain in silence, in silence the shame and the anguish:
Slow, slow he is to put the blame on the love of the woman:
Slow to say she led him astray, swift ever to love and excuse her!
O 'tis a good thing, and I am glad at the seeing,
That man who has all the pain and the patient sorrow and waiting
Keepeth his heart ever young and never upbraideth the woman
For that she laughs in the sun and taketh the joy of her living
And holdeth him to her breast, and knoweth pleasure
And plighteth troth akin to the starry immortals,
And soon forgetteth, and lusteth after another,
And plighteth again, and again, and yet again and again,
And asketh only one thing of man who is patient and loving, —
This: that he swerve not ever, that faithful he be and loyal,
And know that the sorrow of sorrows is only a law of his being,
And all is well with Woman, and the World of Woman, and God,
O 'tis a good thing and I am glad at the seeing!
And this is the rune of man the bearer of pain and sorrow,
The father who giveth the babe his youth his joy and the life of his living!"

(And high in His Heaven God the All-Seeing troubled.)

THE RUNE

O we are weary, how weary, all we of the burthen:
Heavy the breasts with milk that never shall nourish:
Heavy the womb that never again shall be fruitful:
Heavy the hearts that never again shall be weighty.
For we have the burthen upon us, we have the burthen,
The long slow pain, and the sorrow of going, and the parting.
O little hands, O little lips, farewell and farewell:
Bitter the sorrow of bearing only to end with the parting,
Bitter the sorrow of bearing only to end with the parting.

The poems above contain enough information and insight to keep any serious seeker after Faery knowledge busy for a long time. They should also be of interest to any male readers who wish to learn not only more of the Faery lore but also how that relates to the situation of human women throughout the world today.

In the collection of poems published as *Poems and Dramas* there are two individual poems, *Green Branches* and *The Lonely Hunter*, which deal with Joy and Sorrow and which appear to have originally been one. I have taken the liberty of giving them below as one complete poem. The first two verses were published as *Green Branches* and the remainder appeared as *The Lonely Hunter*.

Wave, wave, green branches, wave me far away
To where the forest deepens and the hillside winds, sleeping, stay:
Where Peace doth fold her twilight wings, and through the heart of day
There goes the rumour of passing hours grown faint and grey.

Wave, wave, green branches, my heart like a bird doth hover
Above the nesting-place your green-gloom shadows cover:
O come to my nesting heart, come close, come close, bend over,
Joy of my heart, my life, my prince, my lover!

Green branches, green branches, I see you beckon; I follow!
Sweet is the place you guard, there in the rowan-tree hollow.
There he lies in the darkness, under the frail white flowers,
Heedless at last, in the silence, of these sweet midsummer hours.

But sweeter, it may be, the moss whereon he is sleeping now,
And sweeter the fragrant flowers that may crown his moon-white brow:
And sweeter the shady place deep in an Eden hollow
Wherein he dreams I am with him — and, dreaming, whispers, "Follow!"

Green wind from the green-gold branches, what is the song you bring?
What are all songs for me, now, who no more care to sing?
Deep in the heart of Summer, sweet is life to me still,
But my heart is a lonely hunter that hunts on a lonely hill.

Green is that hill and lonely, set far in a shadowy place;
White is the hunter's quarry, a lost-loved human face:
O hunting heart, shall you find it, with arrow of failing breath,
Led o'er a green hill lonely by the shadowy hound of Death?

Green branches, green branches, you sing of a sorrow olden'
But now it is midsummer weather, earth-young, sunripe, golden:
Here I stand and I wait, here in the rowan-tree hollow,
But never a green leaf whispers, "Follow, oh, Follow, Follow!"

O never a green leaf whispers, where the green-gold branches swing:
O never a song I hear now, where one was wont to sing
Here in the heart of Summer, sweet is life to me still,
But my heart is a lonely hunter that hunts on a lonely hill.

To conclude this chapter on the importance of joy and sorrow I give another poem that has much to reveal concerning Faery insight into these much-misunderstood Faery and human emotions.

Dreams Within Dreams

I have gone out and seen the lands of Faery
And have found sorrow and peace and beauty there,
And have not know one from the other,
But found each
Lovely and gracious alike, delicate and fair.

"They are children of one mother, she that is called Longing,
Desire, Love," one told me: and another,
"her secret name is Wisdom:" and another,
"they are not three but one:"
and another, "touch them not, seek them not, they are wind and flame."

I have come back from the hidden silent lands of Faery
And have forgotten the music of its ancient streams:
And now flame and wind, and the long, grey, wandering wave
And beauty and peace and sorrow are dreams within dreams.

Chapter Eleven

INVOCATION OF PEACE

We are not of the seed of Adam,
But we are the offspring of the Haughty Father.

SOME OF Fiona's most important revelations of Faery lore are contained in a thirty-two line poem called *Invocation of Peace.* To this day you will see sections of it reprinted in books dealing with Celtic mythology where it is often described as being ancient Celtic. In gift shops throughout Scotland you will also find excerpts from it on postcards, mugs, calendars, tea towels etc where it is either unattributed or else will be described as being an ancient Gaelic blessing. It is none of these things. This piece first appeared in the short story *The Amadan* from the collection *Under The Dark Star.* Several of the tales in that book involve the doomed Achanna family, this being the final one. One of the Achanna brothers, Alasdair, has gone mad and hence is known as The Amadan, or Mad One, and Alan Dall is trying to heal him. Alasdair is delirious and muttering in his sleep. Alan asks the sleeping Alasdair,

'Who are they who are about you?' he whispered.
The Amadan turned, and his lips moved. But it was as though others spoke through him —
  'Cha 'n ann do Shiol Adhamh sinn,
  Ach tha sinn de mhuinntir an Athar Uaibhrich.'
  We are not of the seed of Adam,
  But we are the offspring of the Haughty Father.
Alan Dall hesitated. One of the white prayers of Christ was on his lips, but he remembered also the old wisdom of his fathers. So he kneeled, and said a 'seun', [charm] that is strong against the bitter malice of demoniac wiles.

175

Thereafter he put upon him this 'eolas' [knowledge] of healing, touching the brow and heart as he said 'here' and 'here' —
He then recites the *Invocation of Peace*.

Note that it is not Alasdair who answers Alan's question but the spirits that are around him. They make it clear that they are not human, *'We are not of the seed of Adam,'* but are the offspring of the *'Haughty Father.'* This title at first seems like a familiar Gaelic euphemism for God but if these offspring are not human then the Haughty Father who produced them cannot be the God we know. However we know from other tales by Fiona that the title of Haughty Father is given to the dark Faery god Dalua. This is confirmed by a variant on the invocation, a variant that I call the 'Dalua Version,' which is discussed further on. It is said of Dalua that his very shadow brings madness should it fall on you. Judging by the spirits of Dalua who are around Alasdair, this was clearly the cause of his insanity. Note that at first Alan was going to say a white prayer of Christ but when he realised he was dealing with the offspring of Dalua the Haughty Father he changed from uttering a Christian rune to one that came from *'the old wisdom of his fathers.'* This makes it clear that the *Invocation of Peace* is not originally a Christian poem but is much older. Like so many of these pre-Christian runes, much later Christian symbolism has been mingled with the original Faery symbolism. Here the whole push and content is clearly more pre-Christian than it is Christian, as we shall see when we come to consider the Dalua Version shortly. First though, here is the original version as uttered by Alan Dall.

Deep peace I breathe into you,
O weariness, here;
O ache, here!
Deep peace, a soft white dove to you;
Deep peace, a quiet rain to you;
Deep peace, an ebbing wave to you!
Deep peace, red wind of the east from you;
Deep peace, grey wind of the west to you;
Deep peace, dark wind of the north from you;
Deep peace, blue wind of the south to you!
Deep peace, pure red of the flame to you;
Deep peace, pure white of the moon to you;
Deep peace, pure green of the grass to you;

Deep peace, pure brown of the earth to you;
Deep peace, pure grey of the dew to you;
Deep peace, pure blue of the sky to you!
Deep peace of the running wave to you,
Deep peace of the flowing air to you,
Deep peace of the quiet earth to you,
Deep peace of the sleeping stones to you!
Deep peace of the Yellow Shepherd to you,
Deep peace of the Wandering Shepherdess to you,
Deep peace of the Flock of Stars to you,
Deep peace from the Son of Peace to you,
Deep peace from the heart of Mary to you,
From Briget of the Mantle
Deep peace, deep peace!
And with the kindness too of the Haughty Father,
Peace!
In the name of the Three who are One,
And by the will of the King of the Elements,
Peace! Peace!

There is a substantial body of symbolism within these thirty-two lines that requires a good deal of sorting out. First, I would remind you that whenever Fiona used the word 'deep' she meant 'of Faery.' In the Scottish Gaelic language, deep peace is 'domhain sìth' (do=in shee). There is a pun here that is lost in translation, for the word for peace – 'sìth' – is also the word for Faery. The name therefore can be translated as 'Deep Peace', 'Faery Peace' or 'Faery Faery'! So the repeated refrain of *'Deep peace'* is in fact a very emphatic call for the peace of the Faeries. It is only the Faery peace that can overturn the Faery insanity caused by Dalua. The first several invocations of this Faery peace are linked to aspects of the natural world, plus the unique coloured winds from the Realm of Faery. It is only once these powers have been invoked that the Christian symbolism is brought in. But the two are complementary. They sit easily side by side and one is as necessary as is the other.

It is important to take note that the opening line is in the first person. The speaker, in this case Alan Dall, refers to himself as *'I'* and is the source of all the various forms of Faery peace that are given *'to you'*, in this case Alasdair Achanna. In other words, whoever would invoke the Faery peace must allow it to *enter* into, and then *pass out of*, their body and into that of another. This is done, as the opening line reveals, by the passage of breath between the healer and the patient. As this transfer of breath and Faery peace commences, Alan touches his brow when he says the word '*weariness*' and his heart when he says '*ache*.' This emphasis on the negative, along with the deliberate touching of the affected part of the body, has nothing to do with the patient. The healer, Alan, is referring to his own weariness and ache. This is connected with the unique Faery understanding of Joy and Sorrow as discussed in Chapter Ten. In short, the healer's pain (Sorrow) is transferred by the healer's breath into the depths of the patient's being where it is transformed into healing (Joy) and effects the recovery, which, in this case, is the whole point of the invocation.

The third line starts the invocation proper and this is the only line that contains a reference to a non-human living creature, the '*soft white dove*.' This is the symbol for St. Columba whose name, in Gaelic, means a dove. I said above that the Christian symbolism does not appear until later in the invocation, so what about this symbolic reference to St. Columba right at the beginning? Despite the fact he is recognised today as a saint of the Christian faith he is a figure who comfortably straddles the ancient link between the pre-Christian faith and the later teachings of Christ, as has already been discussed. Fiona dealt with him and his dual nature in many of her stories. The reason that he is invoked right at the beginning of this lengthy invocation is because in his Faery aspect he is eminently suited to dealing with the disruptive powers of Dalua.

The next two lines bring in water, first as a '*quiet rain*' and then as an '*ebbing wave*.' As I have repeatedly pointed out in this book, the Realm of Faery is very closely associated with water, the sea, rivers, lochs and so forth, so these two lines are focusing the invocation even more on the Realm of Faery. The next four lines invoke the coloured winds that blow through that realm and which are unknown in our world. These four coloured winds are in a sense the equivalent of the Four Directions as invoked in modern Wiccan rituals and in Western Mystery Tradition ceremonial magic. Each one of these winds brings with it a separate and specific cache of Faery magical symbols and powers that will form the basis of the healing that follows.

The six lines that follow bring in an array of different things: '*flame*,' '*moon*,' '*grass*,' '*earth*,' '*dew*,' and '*sky*' that are all connected with specific colours, just like the four winds in the preceding lines. The important thing here is the colours, and not so much the objects they are connected with. Keeping in mind that the Realm of Faery has no physical substance to it, these colours replace the adjectives that we would use in our world to describe these things. For example, adjectives such as hard, soft, heavy, rough, smooth, dense, malleable etc make sense to us as they relate to a tactile experience of physical objects, but in the Realm of Faery such conditions do not exist. All that exists, to put it simply but crudely, is light. Therefore the adjectives that make most sense there are ones describing the various qualities of light and that of course includes all the colours of the spectrum.

The next four lines do not mention any more colours but they do use three verbs and one adjective, *'running,' 'flowing,' 'sleeping'* and *'quiet,'* that are appropriate both for this world and for the Realm of Faery. More is said on these lines later, in the discussion on the Dalua Version of the invocation as given below.

The last twelve lines introduce eight characters:

the Yellow Shepherd;
the Wandering Shepherdess;
the Son of Peace;
Mary;
Briget of the Mantle;
the Haughty Father;
the Three who are One;
the King of the Elements.

Only two of these, Mary and Briget (or Brigid) of the Mantle, are identifiable people. Mary is exclusively from the Christian tradition but Briget is from the pre-Christian Celtic tradition, as well as the later Christian tradition and the non-human Faery tradition. She is unique in straddling these three traditions. The other six characters are not individual people but rather they are titles. Two of these, the Son of Peace and the King of the Elements, are titles given to Jesus in the Christian tradition, but note that his name is not actually used in the poem. It is perhaps possible that they also relate to a god from the Faery tradition. Two of the other titles used, the Haughty Father and the Three who are One, are commonly given to the Judaic/Christian/Islamic God – *but only in this version of the invocation.* See the comments below regarding the 'Dalua' version for an explanation of this. The other two characters, the Yellow Shepherd and the Wandering Shepherdess, are a god and a goddess from the Faery tradition who are not found in the Christian tradition.

Having said that, there are two passages from *Iona* that may imply an esoteric Christian connection between the Virgin Mary and the Faery Shepherd and Shepherdess. The first one says,

> *"... the three powers who are invoked are St. Micheil ... St. Columba, ... and the Virgin Mary, 'Mathair Uain ghil,' 'Mother of the White Lamb,' as the tender Gaelic has it, who is so beautifully called the golden-haired Virgin Shepherdess."*

The second piece says:

> *"... the old prophecy that Christ shall come again upon Iona, ... now as the Daughter of God, now as the Divine Spirit embodied through mortal birth in a Woman, as once through mortal birth in a Man ... But more wise it is to dream, not of hallowed ground, but of the hallowed gardens of the soul wherein She shall appear white and radiant. Or, that upon the hills, where we are wandered, the Shepherdess shall call us home."*

You can see that these few lines give a very complex but all-encompassing mixture of Faery and Christian characters.

By understanding more of the symbolism contained within the invocation, and by becoming familiar with what this all means, we can quickly see just how powerful an invocation this truly is. But there is more to it. As well as being a spoken and meditative piece for individual use it is also a powerful and well-structured ritual that can be performed in a group setting. In fact it is two rituals, based on the two versions of the invocation. We shall consider the 'Dalua' version in a moment and see how it differs from the original version and why, but for the moment here is some pertinent background information as to how I came to realise the ritualistic nature of the invocation. This is also a good practical example of how Faeries at times communicate important information.

I had been convinced for a long time that this invocation contained within it a complete magical ritual, but whenever I thought over what structure such a ritual might take, I kept hitting brick-walls and dead-ends. Then one summer during three consecutive visits to the Island of Iona over a period of three weeks it all started to open up and reveal itself to me. As stated elsewhere in this book, Iona is a very important place to both the Faeries and to spiritually inclined humans. It is a place that Fiona mentions a lot in her writings and it may well be the place where she first put the *Invocation of Peace* in writing.

I was seated on the raised mound that faces the Abbey of Iona. This is where, by tradition, St. Columba had his cell, and I was wrestling with the problem of how to extract the ritual from the thirty-two lines. I was assuming that any such ritual would take the usual basic shape of a magical ritual with Four Officers of the Quarters, standing or seated in a square formation, and facing a central altar. But this did not feel right. I could not see how the energy could flow in the usual Western Magical Tradition layout. I felt that there was something else to the ritualistic nature of the poem, something deeper and more significant than just the usual fourfold interpretation that magicians of the Western Mystery Tradition tend to apply almost by rote. The second and third times I went back to Iona, seven days apart and seven days after the first visit, I went to the mound again and tried to make some sense of all this.

During my second visit I paid attention to the large slot that is atop St. Columba's Mound. This is explained in the guidebooks as being a stone base with a large, elongated rectangular slot, the purpose of which was to act as the socket for a now lost stone Celtic cross. This vacant slot now serves as an opening into the mound and this seemed very significant. As I gazed down on the mound beneath my feet I felt as if a rush, a torrent, of energy was gushing up through the earth, out through the slot in the stone and into my very being. I was surprised and rather overwhelmed by this but it passed quickly. I sat down on the mound and tried to take in what had just happened but my mind was suddenly so full of answers to my many questions on the possible structure of an *Invocation of Peace* ritual that I had to write them all down before I forgot them.

First, it came to me clearly and strongly that because what we are dealing with here comes from the Realm of Faery it predates our familiar and customary way of working ritual. Yes, the usual fourfold formula can be made to work in this instance but there is another, more ancient way of working lying in the background. If this older way predates our normal Western Mystery Tradition way of doing things then we do not need to follow that formula at all. Why not experiment with a new structure suited to the invocations and power flows that this ritual will invoke? The result of this simple but profound realisation was a sudden in-pouring of yet more ideas and suggestions to my conscious mind which even now, years later, I am still trying to fully untangle and put into words.

It was during my next visit to Iona that I realised that the invocation contains within it not one but two very different rituals. One of them is indeed based on a fourfold pattern, can be performed by a solo magician or with the usual Four Officers, and is based solidly in this world. The main purpose of this ritual is either to make initial contact with the Faery realm or to strengthen an existing Faery contact, thus improving the quality of communication. The ground plan for this version of the ritual *is* the usual Western Mystery Tradition Lodge setting, with the Four Officers situated in the Four Quarters, surrounding a central altar. The usual ritual accoutrements can be used and there are suitable places in the wording of the invocation that allow for meditation and predetermined or spontaneous visualisations.

The thirty-two lines of the poem can be split into eight groups that can be spoken by four Officers in a formal ritual setting. Note that these groupings are conveniently marked in the text by the use of an exclamation mark.

Lines 1 – 3   the formal opening of the ritual;
Lines 4 – 6   the initial blessing;
Lines 7 – 10   the four coloured winds;
Lines 11 – 16   the six colours;
Lines 17 – 20   the first four lines to use the word *'of'* following the Deep Peace invocation;
Lines 21 – 27   a second, deeper invocation to spiritual beings;
Lines 28 – 29   the third and deepest invocation to the Haughty Father;
Lines 30 – 32   the conclusion to the ritual.

In Fiona's story of Alasdair Achanna, the purpose of this ritual was for healing. However its main purpose as far as regular magical group work is concerned is to establish and strengthen Faery contact within the group. With that purpose in mind it could be performed on a regular basis to great advantage. Many possibilities exist as to how to structure the ritual; thanks to the invocation's complexity and fluid symbolism, there is no one correct way. It would be an interesting experiment for each magical group to come up with their own version or versions. Here is just one suggestion which should help you see the breakdown of the possible power-flow within the ritual space.

INVOCATION OF PEACE
(group version)

(Opening)
Officer of the East
Deep peace I breathe into you,
O weariness, here;   (touch brow)
O ache, here!   (touch heart)

(Initial blessing)
Officer of the West
Circumambulate three times, one line spoken on each circumambulation
Deep peace, a soft white dove to you;
Deep peace, a quiet rain to you;
Deep peace, an ebbing wave to you!

(Four coloured winds of Faery)
Officer of the East
Deep peace, red wind of the east from you;   (light candle)

Officer of the West
Deep peace, grey wind of the west to you;   (light candle)

Officer of the North
Deep peace, dark wind of the north from you;   (light candle)

Officer of the South
Deep peace, blue wind of the south to you!   (light candle)

(The purifying colours of Faery)
Officer of the South
Deep peace, pure red of the flame to you;

Officer of the West
Deep peace, pure white of the moon to you;

Officer of the North
Deep peace, pure green of the grass to you;

Officer of the East
Deep peace, pure brown of the earth to you;

Officer of the South
Deep peace, pure grey of the dew to you;

Officer of the North
Deep peace, pure blue of the sky to you!

(Visualisation, led by Officer of the East)

(First invocation)
Officer of the West
Deep peace of the running wave to you,
Deep peace of the flowing air to you,
Deep peace of the quiet earth to you,
Deep peace of the sleeping stones to you!

(Second, deeper invocation)
Officer of the North
Deep peace of the Yellow Shepherd to you,
Deep peace of the Wandering Shepherdess to you,
Deep peace of the Flock of Stars to you,
Deep peace from the Son of Peace to you,
Deep peace from the heart of Mary to you,
From Briget of the Mantle
Deep peace, deep peace!

(Third, and deepest invocation)
Officer of the South
And with the kindness too of the Haughty Father,
Peace!

*(Possible second visualisation – **if it is felt appropriate**)*

(Conclusion)
All Officers
In the name of the Three who are One,
And by the will of the King of the Elements,
Peace! Peace!

Officer of the South   (extinguish candle)
Officer of the East   (extinguish candle)
Officer of the North   (extinguish candle)
Officer of the West   (extinguish candle)

The Dalua Version

The other version of the *Invocation of Peace* is identical to the above except it has the name '*Dalua*' inserted in line 28 – *And with the kindness too of Dalua the Haughty Father.* This changes the basis for the symbolism completely. As we have already learned, the Haughty Father is one of the many titles given to the dark Faery god Dalua. By the simple insertion of this specific name the whole Christian aspect of the invocation is all but removed. By the same token, the whole four-fold structure of the above group ritual becomes inappropriate. It is no longer a ritual based in this world with our familiar four-fold Quarters and Elements. It is now based in the Faery realm where it is only appropriate for a solo *threefold* ritual.

Whereas the main purpose of the ritual given above is to establish or strengthen *group* Faery contacts, the main purpose of this ritual is to allow a deeper level of individual *personal* communication to take place with *existing* Faery contacts than the group ritual can afford. The ritual above is carried out with physical movements, and lines spoken aloud in the physical realm. This version is carried out entirely on an Inner, or meditative, level with no movements in physical space and no lines spoken aloud. The Inner visual image used for this threefold Inner ritual is within a pyramid with only three sides, formed of four equilateral triangles, one as the base and the other three around the magician with the apex above his/her head.

As the magician visualizes him/herself sitting or standing within this three sided pyramid he/she should then go through the Invocation, line by line, and meditate on what each line says and, importantly, how it may relate to any other lines in the poem. This will bring to mind many questions and realisations. It is these questions and realisations that will help reveal the Inner communications being given by the Faery contact. This is important. You will find that each time you perform the Inner ritual there will be new and different connections, and questions come to mind as you ponder over the significance of each line. Pay close attention to these differences, they may well be revealing new information from the Realm of Faery. The first time you try this solo ritual you will realise how much information it already contains but you will also find dozens of questions coming to mind.

I would suggest that on closing each Inner working you immediately write down as much as you can remember and in as much detail as you can recall. As time progresses you will be able to see changes, patterns, repeating motifs etc emerging with each successive performance. These changes will bear the core of your Faery communications. You will need to study them and ponder over them frequently in order to get the most of the time and effort this Inner ritual demands.

As an example of the types of things that came to mind to me the first time I tried this solo ritual I give below some extracts from the diary I kept specifically for this purpose. This should give you an idea of just how much symbolism and complexity is woven into these thirty-two lines.

INVOCATION OF PEACE
(Dalua/solo version)

1   *Deep peace I breathe into you,*

2   *O weariness, here;*

3   *O ache, here!*

4   *Deep peace, a soft white dove to you;*

5   *Deep peace, a quiet rain to you;*

6   *Deep peace, an ebbing wave to you!*

7   *Deep peace, red wind of the east from you;*

8   *Deep peace, grey wind of the west to you;*

9   *Deep peace, dark wind of the north from you;*

10   *Deep peace, blue wind of the south to you!*

11   *Deep peace, pure red of the flame to you;*

12   *Deep peace, pure white of the moon to you;*

13   *Deep peace, pure green of the grass to you;*

14   *Deep peace, pure brown of the earth to you;*

15   *Deep peace, pure grey of the dew to you;*

16   *Deep peace, pure blue of the sky to you!*

17   Deep peace of the running wave to you,
18   Deep peace of the flowing air to you,
19   Deep peace of the quiet earth to you,
20   Deep peace of the sleeping stones to you!
21   Deep peace of the Yellow Shepherd to you,
22   Deep peace of the Wandering Shepherdess to you,
23   Deep peace of the Flock of Stars to you,
24   Deep peace from the Son of Peace to you,
25   Deep peace from the heart of Mary to you,
26   From Briget of the Mantle
27   Deep peace, deep peace!
28   And with the kindness too of Dalua the Haughty Father,
29   Peace!
30   In the name of the Three who are One,
31   And by the will of the King of the Elements,
32   Peace! Peace!

Line 1 – who is the speaker? This is the only line that says '...*into you*' as opposed to all the others which say '...*to you.*' The speaker therefore actually breathes into you (and who exactly is '*you*' meant to be?) whereas everything else is given to you.

Lines 2 & 3 – we know from the original story that when the speaker recited these two lines he touched first the brow and then the heart when he spoke the word '*here*'. The use of the exclamation '*O*' at the start of both lines implies sadness, fatigue or desperation. The use of '*weariness*' and '*ache*' imply the completion of a long journey, hard labour or some other long, tiring physical activity.

Line 4 – '*white*' is used and then repeated on a 'higher' level as '*pure white*' in Line 12. The '*dove*' is the Faery St Columba.

Line 5 – the word '*quiet*' (describing *rain*) is repeated in Line 19 (describing *earth*).

Line 6 – the phrase *'ebbing wave'*, implying weakness of motion, is repeated on a 'higher' level in Line 17 where it becomes a *'running wave'* implying strength in motion. This is the first of four lines (Lines 17, 18 and 20) that use verbs to describe their subject.

Line 7 – *'red'* is used and then repeated on a 'higher' level as *'pure red'* in Line 11. This is one of only two lines (the other being Line 9) that say *'from you'* as opposed to the usual *'to you.'*

Line 8 – *'grey'* is used and then repeated on a 'higher' level as *'pure grey'* in Line 15.

Line 9 – the word *'dark'* is used to describe a wind but this is the only one of the colours of the four winds that is not given on a 'higher' level in Lines 11 – 16. It is also the second line to use *'from you'* instead of *'to you'*; the other occurrence is Line 7.

Line 10 – *'blue'* is used and then repeated on a 'higher' level as *'pure blue'* in Line 16.

Lines 7 – 10 are the four coloured winds from the four directions. Two of them, Lines 7 and 9, come from you in the East and North respectively, whereas the other two, Lines 8 and 10, move to you in the West and South respectively. Lines 24, 25 and 26 also use *'from'*.

Lines 11 – 16 use six colours to describe various things. Four of these colours are the 'higher' levels of the same colours named in Lines 4, 7, 8 and 10. The other two colours, *'pure green'* (Line 13) and *'pure brown'* (Line 14) occur for the first time. Note that these are 'earth' colours, or perhaps colours with deeper meaning to the Faeries.

Line 17 – second of the lines to use a verb, *'running'*, which is the 'higher' version of the verb *'ebbing'* used in Line 6.

Line 18 – third of the lines to use a verb, *'flowing'*, which is not repeated anywhere else.

Line 19 – does not use a verb despite being sandwiched between lines that do. It uses the word *'quiet'* that otherwise only appears in Line 5.

Line 20 – last of the four 'verb' lines, the verb here being '*sleeping*'.

Line 21 – contains the only use of '*Yellow*' and mentions a Faery god, the '*Yellow Shepherd*'.

Line 22 – mentions a Faery goddess, the '*Wandering Shepherdess*' who may be an aspect of the Virgin Mary.

Line 23 – Mentions a '*Flock*' of stars (unusual collective noun for stars – significant!) Is this the 'flock' that the shepherd and shepherdess, mentioned above, look after?

Line 24 – first of three consecutive lines to use '*from*' a person. The person in this case being the '*Son of Peace*', or Christ, that connects with the title given in Line 30.

Line 25 – second line to use '*from*', this time from Mary, the first of only three people mentioned by name.

Line 26 – third and last line to use '*from*', this time from Briget, the second of only three people to be mentioned by name, but the usual '*to you*' is not used.

Line 27 – the only line where '*Deep peace*' is repeated and the only line where '*Deep peace*' is not followed by any other words.

Line 28 – the third line to use a specific name, '*Dalua*', and like Line 26, the familiar '*to you*' is missing. The title '*Haughty Father*' refers not to the Christian God but to Dalua who created the offspring that are not of the seed of Adam – the Faeries. We know this from the original story in which the poem appeared.

Line 29 – first of only two lines, the other being Line 32, where the word '*peace*' is used without the usual '*Deep*' preceding it.

Line 30 – the title '*Three who are One*' could refer to the Christian God, but considering what we know from Line 28, it seems more likely that this is referring to a triple-aspect of the Faery god Dalua.

Line 31 – the title *'King of the Elements'* refers to Christ and makes a connection with Line 24 where another title for Christ is used.

Line 32 – the final line and the only place other than Line 29 where the word *'peace'* is used without the word *'Deep'* preceding it, indicating that everything has now left the Faery Realm and has been brought down to our earthly level. It is also the only line where the word *'peace'* is repeated.

Where, you may ask, is the important Faery lore revealed in the above collection of connections and associations? It isn't! There is none there. But that is OK. This was what came to me the first time I tried the solo ritual within the Inner three-sided pyramid. The following times I repeated the ritual I found my attention focusing not on the whole invocation but on small sections of it. These started to reveal symbolism and connections that are not mentioned in the thirty-two lines and these new symbols and connections in turn led on to a deeper understanding of passages in Fiona Macleod's writings that I had previously ignored or missed as I had considered them to be unimportant. *That* is where the Faery lore itself was then revealed. However, to get to that point of revelation, it is necessary for your mind to have a real grasp of the structure of the invocation, and how some lines seem to be connected to other lines elsewhere in the poem.

Appendix

THE MAIN WORKS OF FIONA MACLEOD

The original titles and publication dates of Fiona Macleod's main works are given below, but it should be noted that most of them were reprinted several times in different combinations during William's life and for several years after his death. Several foreign publishers also published many editions and these are often different from their British originals. Not only were the collections of tales in each volume switched from one to another but the text of many of them was also edited and amended on subsequent editions, resulting in a confusing mixture of editions and versions.

Pharais: A Romance of the Isles Frank Murray, Derby, 1894. Reprinted by T.N. Foulis, Edinburgh, 1907.

The Mountain Lovers John Lane, London, 1895. Second edition John Lane, London & New York, 1906.

The Sin-Eater and Other Tales Patrick Geddes & Colleagues, Edinburgh, 1895. Reprinted David Nutt, London, 1899.

The Washer of the Ford and other Legendary Moralities Patrick Geddes & Colleagues, Edinburgh, 1896. Reprinted David Nutt, London, 1899.

Reissue of the Shorter Tales of Fiona Macleod Patrick Geddes & Colleagues, Edinburgh, 1896. Reprinted David Nutt, London, 1899.
Volume 1 – Spiritual Tales
Volume 2 – Barbaric Tales
Volume 3 – Tragic Romances

Green Fire: A Romance Archibald, Constable & Co., Westminster, 1896.

From The Hills of Dream: Mountain Songs and Island Runes Patrick Geddes & Colleagues, Edinburgh, 1896.

The Laughter of Peterkin: A Retelling of the Old Tales of the Celtic Wonderland Archibald, Constable & Co., Westminster, 1897.

The Dominion of Dreams Archibald, Constable & Co., Westminster, 1899. Reprinted Constable & Co., 1909.

The Divine Adventure: Iona: By Sundown Shores: Studies in Spiritual History Chapman and Hall, Ltd., London, 1900.

Wind and Wave: Selected Tales Bernhard Tauchnitz, Leipzig, 1902.

The Winged Destiny: Studies in the Spiritual History of the Gael Chapman and Hall, Ltd., London, 1904.

The Sunset of Old Tales Bernhard Tauchnitz, Leipzig, 1905.

Where the Forest Murmurs: Nature Essays Georges Newnes, Ltd., New York, 1906.

From the Hills of Dream: Threnodies and Songs and Later Poems William Heinemann, London, 1907.

The Immortal Hour: a Drama in Two Acts T.N. Foulis, London, 1908.

A Little Book of Nature T.N. Foulis, Edinburgh and London, 1909.

The Works of "Fiona Macleod" Uniform Edition, London, Heinemann, 1910. Arranged by Mrs. William Sharp.
   Volume 1 – "Pharais" and "The Mountain Lovers"
   Volume 2 – "The Sin-Eater" and "The Washer of the Ford"
   Volume 3 – The Dominion of Dreams: Under the Dark Star
   Volume 4 – The Divine Adventure: Iona. Studies in Spiritual History
   Volume 5 – The Winged Destiny: Studies in the Spiritual History of the Gael
   Volume 6 – The Silence of Amor: Where the Forest Murmurs
   Volume 7 – Poems and Dramas

Readers interested in studying the complete texts of Fiona Macleod's output should take note of Elizabeth's comments in the Foreword to Volume One of this set: "*Into this collected edition are gathered all the writings of William Sharp published under his pseudonym "Fiona Macleod", <u>which he cared to have preserved</u> … I have carefully followed the author's written and spoken instructions as to selection, <u>deletion</u> and arrangement. To the preliminary arrangement he gave much thought, especially to the <u>revision of the text</u>, and he made <u>considerable changes</u> in the later versions of certain of the poems and tales.*" (Emphasis added.)

In other words, it is necessary to go to the original printings of many of these works in order to read them in their entirety. For ease of reference here is a list of the contents of each volume:

Volume 1: *Pharais – The Mountain Lovers* contains a foreword by Elizabeth plus the first two novels *Pharais* and *The Mountain Lovers*. A bibliographical note follows these on the dates and publishers of the first editions. All of the following volumes in the set contain relevant bibliographical notes.

Volume 2: *The Sin Eater – The Washer of the Ford* contains *The Sin Eater* with its *Prologue – From Iona*, plus several short stories: *The Sin-Eater; The Ninth Wave; The Judgment o' God; The Harping of Cravetheen; Silk o' the Kine* plus *Ula and Urla* which was not in the original edition. Alongside these are the tales originally published as *The Washer of the Ford* with the *Prologue* followed by *The Washer of the Ford; St. Bride of the Isles; The Fisher of Men; The Last Supper; The Dark Nameless One; The Three Marvels of Hy; The Woman with the Net; Cathal of the Woods* plus *The Song of the Sword; The Flight of the Culdees; Mircath; The Sad Queen* (not in the original edition); *The Laughter of Scathach the Queen; Ahez the Pale* (not in the original edition); *The King of Ys and Dahut the Red* (not in the original edition).

Volume 3: *The Dominion of Dreams – Under the Dark Star* contains the tales from *The Dominion of Dreams*: *Dalua; By the Yellow Moonrock; Lost; Morag of the Glen; The Sight; The Dark Hour of Fergus; The Hills of Ruel; The Archer; The Birdeen; The Book of the Opal; The Wells of Peace; In the Shadow of the Hills; The Distant Country; A Memory of Beauty; Enya of the Dark Eyes; The Crying of Wind; Honey of the Wild Bees; The Birds of Emar; Ulad of the Dreams; The Wind, The Shadow, and the Soul.* Also in this volume are the tales from *Under The Dark Star: The Anointed Man; The Dan-nan-Ron; Green Branches; Children of the Dark Star; Alasdair the Proud* and *The Amadan*.

Volume 4: *The Divine Adventure – Iona – Studies in Spiritual History* contains the whole of *The Divine Adventure* and the essay originally published simply as *Iona*. Alongside these two works are the tales originally published as *By Sundown Shores*, namely *By Sundown Shores; The Wind, Silence, and Love; Barabal: A Memory; The White Heron; The Smoothing of the Hand; The White Fever; The Sea-Madness; Earth, Fire, and Water*. These are joined by two extracts from *Green Fire* which are here called *The Herdsman* and *Fragments*. The volume concludes with the short piece *A Dream*.

Volume 5: *The Winged Destiny: Studies in the Spiritual History of the Gael* includes *The Sunset of Old Tales; The Treud Nan Ron; The Man on the Moor; The Woman at the Cross-Ways; The Lords of Wisdom; The Wayfarer; Queens of Beauty; Orpheus and Oisin; The Awakening of Angus Òg; Children of Water; Cuilidh Mhoire; Sea-Magic; Fara-a-Ghaol; Sorrow on the Wind; The Lynn of Dreams; Maya; Prelude; Celtic; The Gaelic Heart; The Gael and his Heritage; Seumas: A Memory; Aileen: A Memory; The Four Winds of Eirinn; Two Old Songs of May; "The Shadowy Waters"; A Triad; The Ancient Beauty* and *The Winged Destiny*.

Volume 6: *The Silence of Amor – Where the Forest Murmurs* contains the two pieces *The Silence of Amor* and *Tragic Landscapes* plus a collection of short pieces, here called *Where The Forest Murmurs* and individually as *Where the Forest Murmurs; The Mountain Charm; The Clans of the Grass; The Tides; The Hill-Tarn; At the Turn of the Year; The Sons of the North Wind; St. Briget of the Shores; The Heralds of March; The Tribe of the Plover; The Awakener of the Woods; The Wild-Apple; Running Waters; The Summer Heralds; The Sea-Spell; Summer Clouds; The Cuckoo's Silence; The Coming of Dusk; At the Rising of the Moon; The Gardens of the Sea; The Milky Way; September; The Children of Wind and the Clan of Peace; Still Waters; The Pleiad-Month; The Rainy Hyades; Winter Stars I; Winter Stars II; Beyond the Blue Septentrions. Two Legends of the Polar Stars; White Weather: A Mountain Reverie; Rosa Mystica (and Roses of Autumn); The Star of Rest: A Fragment* and *An Almanac*.

Volume 7: *Poems and Dramas* contains twenty eight poems collected under the title *Poems*; sixteen poems collected under the title *Closing Doors*; four poems collected under the title *From the Heart of a Woman*; thirty eight poems collected under the title *Foam of the Past*; twenty poems collected under the title *Through the Ivory Gate*, five poems collected under the title *The Dirge of the Four Cities* and thirty one poems collected under the title of *The Hour of Beauty*. The volume concludes with a *Foreword* concerning the two plays *The Immortal Hour* and *The House of Usna;* both plays are then reproduced in full. Following Elizabeth Sharp's usual bibliographical note there is a sonnet called *Fiona Macleod* by Alfred Noyes.

Volume 8, which is only available in the 'Pocket Edition' of the collected works, is entitled *The Laughter of Peterkin* and contains a *Prologue. The Laughter of Peterkin* is followed by *The Four White Swans; The Fate of the Sons of Turenn; Darthool and the Sons of Usna* and concludes with *Notes* on the sources used for these retellings of old Celtic tales plus a glossary of the Gaelic names and words contained therein.

William Sharp and Fiona Macleod both contributed essays, poems, criticisms and articles to many of the literary and art journals, anthologies and magazines of the day. Included in these are *The Canterbury Series, Camelot Classics, The Art Journal, The Academy, The Literary World, Literature, The Realm, The Young Folks' Paper, The Glasgow Herald, The Athenaeum, Modern Thought, Harper, The Fortnightly Review, Good Words, New York Independent, Atlantic Monthly, Nineteenth Century, Pall Mall Magazine, Century, Country Life, Theosophical Review, Dome, Contemporary Review* and *The North American Review.*

In the second volume of her two-volume set *William Sharp (Fiona Macleod) A Memoir* (William Heinemann, London, 1912) Elizabeth Sharp gives full details of all of these pieces, many of which were never reprinted anywhere else.

INDEX

Lightning Source UK Ltd.
Milton Keynes UK
UKOW042207150413

209269UK00003B/674/P